HOSPITALITY BRANDING

The large body of research published by scholars in the dynamic field of hospitality management has been slow to find its way into the classroom and the strategic, managerial, and operating practices of the hospitality industry. In the new series Cornell Hospitality Management: Best Practices, Cornell University Press will publish short books that present, in distilled form, current research findings on best practices in the hospitality industry. As recognized experts, the volume editors are ideally qualified to identify the best available research and present it in a thoughtful and coherent way that serves both the pedagogical needs of the classroom and the practical needs of the hospitality industry. The first books in the series will address hospitality branding, human resource management, finance, operations and revenue management, food and beverage management, and design.

CORNELL
HOSPITALITY
MANAGEMENT
BEST PRACTICES

Edited by CHEKITAN S. DEV

HOSPITALITY BRANDING

CHEKITAN S. DEV

CORNELL UNIVERSITY PRESS
ITHACA AND LONDON

First published 2012 by Cornell University Press
First printing, Cornell Paperbacks, 2012

Printed in the United States of America

Library of Congress Cataloging-in-Publication Data
Dev, Chekitan S. (Chekitan Singh), 1959–
    Hospitality branding / Chekitan S. Dev.
        p. cm.
    Includes bibliographical references and index.
    ISBN 978-0-8014-7819-2 (pbk. : alk. paper) — ISBN 978-0-8014-5203-1 (cloth)
    1. Hospitality industry—Marketing.   2. Branding (Marketing)   I. Title.
    TX911.3.M3D48   2012
    338.4'7910688—dc23   2012024820

Cornell University Press strives to use environmentally responsible suppliers and materials to the fullest extent possible in the publishing of its books. Such materials include vegetable-based, low-VOC inks and acid-free papers that are recycled, totally chlorine-free, or partly composed of nonwood fibers. For further information visit our website at www.cornellpress.cornell.edu.

Cloth printing   10 9 8 7 6 5 4 3 2 1
Paperback printing   10 9 8 7 6 5 4 3 2 1

Contents

Preface

This book distills the essence of my thinking about hospitality marketing and branding and brings the results of my academic work to a wider audience that I hope will benefit from its insights. Its contents cover over twenty years of scholarly labor, presenting studies undertaken with the help of many collaborators, whose contributions I have acknowledged elsewhere in the book. Although the chapters are organized around four general themes, taken together they represent an evolution in hospitality marketing and branding studies that has brought the development and management of the *brand* squarely into the spotlight as the focal point of theoretical analysis and industry success.

Today scholars and industry leaders view branding in a new light. Whereas hospitality business strategy once began with marketing and incorporated branding as one of its elements, such strategy now begins with branding and incorporates marketing within the larger enterprise. The brand has become not only the chief means of attracting customers; it has, more broadly, become the chief organizing principle for most hospitality organizations.

Over the past two decades, industry observers and the public alike have witnessed an explosion of brands in every market segment and in every sector, from hotels to restaurants to resorts to cruise lines. As a result the consumer can be easily overwhelmed by a sea of sameness in which it is increasingly difficult to distinguish one brand from another, one positioning approach from another, one splashy media campaign from another. Brands unceasingly search for the latest marketing hook and fall all over themselves to catch the consumer's eye—and wallet.

This never-ending quest for market share follows trend after trend, from offering ever more elaborate and sophisticated amenities to novel, cross-sectoral brand affiliations to the use of social media as a marketing tool—all driven by the preeminence of the brand. Hospitality firms today use their brand identities to generate brand value, hoping to leverage the presence of a brand in the marketplace to attract customers, breed customer loyalty, and, ideally, create passionate lifelong brand champions.

This book captures the most critical developments in the quest for brand value. Each of its four parts includes presentations of empirical studies followed by a related case study offering an important application or illustration of that part's theme. Part I, "The Hospitality Brandscape," begins in chapter 1 with an overview of hospitality marketing and branding studies over the past two decades and a look forward to the trends that will define the next decade. That is followed in chapter 2 with the highlights of a brand roundtable held at Cornell University's Center for Hospitality Research in which industry leaders and leading scholars shared ideas about the use of branding to drive business survival and success. Chapter 3 then presents an analysis of the use of Internet flash sales to market hotel stays. Part I closes with a case study reviewing the efforts of Carnival Cruise lines to differentiate itself in the burgeoning cruise market and offering suggestions for branding success.

Part II, "Global Branding," features three studies that offer insights on effective strategic approaches to branding in the era of globalization. Chapter 4 discusses and analyzes strategies for global market entry; chapter 5 compares the merits of franchising and management contracting; and chapter 6, acknowledging the trend toward adopting a market orientation in global branding, analyzes the choice between a competitor orientation and a customer orientation. The case study for part II presents the main outlines of a fascinating legal case, summarizing the issues involved in a lawsuit brought by a Ritz-Carlton hotel owner against the parent brand, which had placed a co-branded resort carrying the Bulgari name (guided by Ritz-Carlton and initially promoted as such) on the island of Bali.

Part III, "Strategic Branding," delves more deeply into branding as strategy. Chapter 7 introduces an approach to managing brand equity using a system that measures such equity quantitatively. Brands using this technique would be able to assess their brand equity more effectively. Chapter 8 offers an analytical framework with which brand marketers can assess and manage their market positioning within a competitive set by mapping that position on a four-quadrant grid. Part III also includes, in chapter 9, an analysis of the use of brand extensions to generate customer loyalty. The case study for part III describes an effort by a property under the Taj brand in Goa to undertake service innovation as a means of upgrading a property's market position.

Part IV, "Branding Execution," offers three studies that examine the relationships that hotel brands develop with the properties that carry their brand names directly to the customer. To manage the use of its brand image to attract customers to its properties, a brand must develop effective relationships—brand partnerships—with its property owners and managers. Chapter 10 argues that understanding how to reduce or eliminate opportunism is best approached from a relational exchange perspective rather than from a transaction cost perspective. Chapter 11 reports evidence that franchisor-franchisee relationships work best when both parties communicate openly and interact harmoniously in a strong partnership. The study presented in chapter 12 shows evidence that brand partners can reduce opportunism by adhering to a set of relational norms. Finally, the part IV case study follows a small tour operator offering winery tours in the Finger Lakes region of New York State as it weighs the benefits and costs of partnering with the online marketing brand Groupon.

The purpose of this book is to make all these findings from scholarly research available to anyone with an interest in hospitality management and marketing, particularly those who appreciate the role that branding has assumed. It strikes a balance between the wisdom of recent history and the cutting-edge promise of future trends. While the principles recommended here might not guarantee survival or success, the research shows that they can provide a competitive advantage to hospitality brands seeking to survive and thrive in an increasingly cluttered brand world.

▶ PART ONE ◀

THE HOSPITALITY BRANDSCAPE

CHAPTER ONE

Hospitality Marketing and Branding: Past and Future

Hospitality marketing helps businesses provide real value to targeted customers, motivate purchase, and ultimately solve customer problems. Creating customer value and satisfaction are at the heart of hospitality and travel industry marketing. While many factors contribute to making a business successful, the most successful companies at all levels are strongly customer focused and heavily committed to marketing.

Against this backdrop of marketing preeminence, this chapter discusses the evolution of hospitality marketing over the past fifty years, at a moment coinciding with the fiftieth anniversary of the *Cornell Hospitality Quarterly (CHQ)*, by reviewing key marketing developments by decade, particularly as seen through the pages of the *CHQ*. The chapter closes by exploring the possibilities the next decade offers.[1]

Methodology

In an attempt to "triangulate" our analysis by using multiple sources of data, we completed this study using three unrelated sources. First, we used Google Scholar to conduct a citation analysis of all hospitality marketing articles published in the *CHQ* over the past fifty years to reveal the most influential *CHQ* articles in each decade. Second, we obtained marketing spending data from PKF Hospitality Research to reveal trends by decade. Third, we used an informal e-mail survey of industry and academic experts who were invited to provide insight into the most influential people, practices, and papers in each decade. Then we merged the data from the three sources we tapped (Google Scholar, PKF, and the experts) to present our findings by decade.

1960s: Promotion, Promotion, Promotion

Developments in technology and marketing drove rapid changes in the hospitality industry in the 1960s. The founding and development of several national hotel chains brought on new standards and dramatically increased competition. From a marketing perspective, based on a review of *CHQ* marketing-related articles and experts' opinions, *promotion* was the prevailing theme.

The February 1964 *CHQ* published three full chapters of C. Dewitt Coffman's landmark book on hotel promotions, *The Full House: A Hotel/Motel Promotion Primer*.[2] The book was devoured by hotel owners, managers, and marketers and quickly became required reading in hospitality marketing courses. Coffman was not alone among marketing and promotion-minded luminaries. According to the *CHQ* survey, Curt Carlson, Kemmons Wilson, Conrad Hilton, Adrian Philips, and Bill Marriott—whose names are synonymous with hotel development and promotion—had the greatest impact on hospitality marketing in the 1960s.

During the 1960s marketing evolved into a discipline with its own set of theories, principles, and tools, beginning with the coining by Harvard Business School professor Neil Borden of the term "marketing mix." Soon thereafter another Harvard professor, E. Jerome McCarthy, suggested the four elements of the marketing mix, the now-famous "4 Ps": product, price, place, and promotion. Marketing-related articles found in early issues of *CHQ* have confirmed that the last element, *promotion*, was the most important marketing practice of the decade.

David Dorf wrote one of the first marketing-related articles published in the *CHQ*.[3] Dorf expounded on the importance of package plans that would attract travelers looking for economical, planned vacations. Published that same year, an article by H. Victor Grohman made availability and accessibility to customers the key to successfully organizing the operation and space of a hotel.[4]

CHQ articles of the 1960s by Robert Bliss and Edward Bursk underlined the primary importance of promotional marketing and insisted on its powerful future.[5] William Morton followed up on Bursk's article, cautioning hotel managers that refusing to adopt marketing as a new business philosophy is tantamount to "shutting your door not only to opportunity—but barring your own survival" (9).[6]

The 1960s was also the decade when technology met promotion. Introduced in 1965 by Holiday Inn, Holidex was the first automated hotel reservation system and it revolutionized hotel operations. The *CHQ* itself marked this revolution, praising systems that could instantaneously guarantee room reservations at a set price.[7] These new systems dramatically decreased no-shows and virtually eliminated the need for overbooking.

1970s: Product Development and Market Research

Innovative developments of the 1960s, such as Holidex and John Portman's radical new hotel designs, set the stage for marketing activity and growth in the 1970s and beyond. Innovations in reservations technology and the development of many new hotel brands propelled the industry as customer expectations changed rapidly. Smart hoteliers had to work hard to keep pace. This review of *CHQ* marketing articles of the 1970s found that *product development* and *market research* were the predominant themes.

The work of Michael Leven, who was hired from Americana Hotels to become the CEO of Days Inn, indicates the importance of marketing knowledge during the 1970s. With Leven at the helm, Days Inn more than doubled its portfolio of hotels and rooms after he introduced a program showing Days Inn management and employees the importance of a customer orientation. Under Leven, employees were rewarded—never penalized—for taking the initiative to help a customer. According to Leven, "Service falls short when employees are always trying to please their immediate boss. You end up putting layers between yourself and the customer."[8]

In the 1970s hospitality marketers recognized the need for product development as a long-range corporate strategy. It became clearer that hospitality establishments had to be constantly adjusting the product to changing tastes, technologies, and competition. Portman's innovative architecture radically changed the look and feel of contemporary hotels and, more to the point, gave permission to others to experiment with hotel design. Portman's designs—such as restaurants revolving atop skyscrapers—also revolutionized hotel restaurants by blending architecture and technology.

CHQ articles in the 1970s by Graham Campbell-Smith, William Swinyard, and Charles Ramond reflected these developments in marketing the restaurant experience, providing a comprehensive overview of the state of restaurant marketing and guiding managers in the use of customer research for advertising and product development to enhance customer satisfaction.[9] Other top articles from the 1970s analyzed marketing research for hotels in considerable detail; notable examples were a piece by Clarence Peters and two written by Peter Yesawich, who was included in the list of the most influential hospitality marketers of the decade, along with the aforementioned Michael Leven, as well as W. W. "Bud" Grice and marketing researchers Peter Drucker and Robert Lewis.[10]

1980s: Revenue Management and Brand Development

Scholarly interest in *CHQ* marketing articles increased dramatically during the 1980s, culminating near the end of the decade in the revolutionary concepts of *revenue management* and *branding.* Articles by Eric Orton, Walter Relihan, and Sheryl Kimes explained the basic theory and mechanics of the concept and showed hospitality managers how they could employ revenue management techniques in their businesses.[11]

Revenue management, which had already spread across the airline industry, would significantly alter the hospitality industry's sales practices. Its sophisticated mathematical techniques put new demands on data resources, requiring analysts with detailed market knowledge to work with advanced computing systems. Many large business-class and luxury hotels added full-time revenue managers to their staffs. The ability to maximize revenue became such an important management tool that today it is not unheard of to find corporate vice presidents of marketing whose careers started as revenue managers.

Our survey revealed, however, that the most influential industry people of the 1980s were not revenue managers but visionary leaders who led their companies into new territories of brand development and brand management. Gerard Pelisson, Paul Dubrule, Ian Schrager, Bill Marriott, Horst Schulze, and Isadore Sharp were the names cited by survey respondents. A recent study notes, "If we review the concept of branding, it's really about communicating values, mission, and vision of the company to the employees and customer."[12]

This branding trend made the 1980s the decade of *brand development,* producing the greatest number of new brands and brand extensions in hotel business history. This was also the decade of a new industry phenomenon, brands with numerous tiers, initiated by Robert Hazard and Gerald Pettit, of Quality International (later Choice International). The ensuing decades continued to witness the unveiling of new brands, but not to the extent that was seen during the 1980s.

1990s: Customer Satisfaction and Loyalty

Conventional marketing wisdom says that it costs five times as much to create a new customer as it does to maintain a current one. Bill Marriott is credited with saying that it costs ten dollars to bring a guest into a Marriott Hotel the first time but only one dollar in special effort to persuade that guest to return. This wisdom became particularly critical following the profligate brand development activity of the 1980s.

CHQ marketing-related articles of the 1990s reflected this trend, focusing on keeping customers in the face of new and greater competition. The most influential marketing articles of the decade were about *customer satisfaction* and *customer loyalty*. For example, John Bowen and Stowe Shoemaker's 1998 empirical study of customer loyalty showed that loyal customers are less price sensitive than other customers are, that they will spend more on food and beverage and other services, and, most important, that they will generate additional business for a hotel through positive word of mouth.[13] Laurette Dubé and Leo Renaghan produced a large-sample study that compared chain preferences with specific chain attributes. Their article identified industry best practices as these relate to customer loyalty and, in so doing, discovered—to the surprise of many managers—features that customers valued more highly than managers did.[14] Other prominent articles exploring loyalty were written by Richard Labagh and Jonathan Barsky; Dubé, Renaghan, and Jane Miller; and Atila Yüksel and Mike Rimmington.[15]

Customer relationship management (CRM) became a buzz term during the 1990s. The CRM phenomenon was generated by additions to the body of research knowledge and the development of automated guest history programs. Four Seasons had begun developing its "Greetings" system at individual properties as early as 1986, although it was not rolled out systemwide until the 1990s.[16] Other chains quickly followed suit in developing their own proprietary programs.

The most influential people in hospitality marketing during the 1990s, the survey revealed, included John Bowen. During the 1990s Bowen produced not only the widely cited abovementioned article with Stowe Shoemaker, but also a textbook, now standard issue, with Philip Kotler and James Makens. This textbook is as popular in hospitality marketing classes today as were C. Dewitt Coffman's books in the 1960s and 1970s. Other individuals cited by our survey included hoteliers Barry Sternlicht, Frank Camacho, Bill Kimpton, Steve Wynn, and Sol Kerzner. These hospitality leaders were all responsible for important innovations and developments that advanced the industry's customer focus.

The decade of the 1990s was focused on generating research to better understand customers, develop closer relationships with them, retain them as loyal customers, and secure a lifetime stream of income from them. The Internet came to prominence in 1995, and over the balance of the 1990s an anxious industry and an apprehensive public haltingly learned how to use it. It was clear that this new medium would benefit those who could harness its great power, although the public had not yet been fully convinced as the new millennium approached.

2000s: Internet Marketing Comes of Age

The predominant theme for the 2000s was *web marketing,* but many marketing-related articles of the new decade continued to mine the customer focus theme of the 1990s, focusing on customer loyalty and CRM. Seymus Baloglu's study of customer loyalty programs in a Las Vegas casino was one of the most cited of the decade, while Jonathan Barsky and Leonard Nash analyzed customer emotions as they relate to satisfaction and loyalty.[17]

Several articles continued the discussion about the use of the Internet that began in the late 1990s. Peter O'Connor and Andrew Frew surveyed electronic distribution managers from major brands and reviewed what were considered to be the most important hotel marketing channels at the time, going on to project future developments.[18] Roland Schegg, Susanne Frey, Jamie Murphy, and Doina Olaru reviewed customer response via website and e-mail in their study of electronic presence and communications in a sample of two hundred Swiss hotels.[19] Sunmee Choi and Sheryl Kimes created a fictitious business hotel with a simulated revenue management system to analyze the effectiveness of various electronic distribution channels.[20]

Industry educators and practitioners returned education to the forefront, naming Bob Gilbert and Kaye Chon among the most influential people of the decade.

2010s: Data-Driven Marketing

As we move into the 2010s, hospitality marketers face new challenges and opportunities. For example, marketing communications is forever changed, with the Internet and social media favored by tech savvy people born in the late 1970s and beyond. Google searches and text messaging are de rigueur, with instant response expected; traditional means of communication no longer work. Moreover, coupling the new mobile marketing technologies with tracking devices enabled with radio frequency identification (RFID) and global positioning system (GPS) makes it possible to target markets with unprecedented precision. Research that can discover and refine effective marketing communication techniques for those entering their thirties and the generations to follow is sorely needed.

Social media sites that were important and popular a few years ago (Yahoo, MySpace, eBay) are declining, while other sites have burst forth (Facebook, Twitter, YouTube). As new sites develop and special interest groups that relate to travel grow we will need to better understand how to effectively and efficiently interact with these groups. We believe that an inflection point occurred in March 2010, when Facebook surpassed the leader, Google, in market share.

Servicescapes are being transformed to fit parts of the day. A public space that accommodates breakfast will not serve the needs of someone looking for a relaxing lounge upon returning to a hotel after a stressful day away from home. As the *CHQ* has emphasized regarding restaurants, hospitality venues must borrow concepts from theater and change the "stage" to provide guests with the environment that best suits their needs. Courtyard by Marriott has developed a homelike environment in a central public area that encourages people to leave their rooms for a common space in which to send e-mails, read, finish reports, and socialize. Research in the 2010s will surely focus on the effective use of servicescapes to offer a better product.

Concern for the environment is here to stay, and hotel marketing, architecture, and engineering will develop new products that reduce hotels' environmental impact and enhance sustainability and health. This decade will see rooms drawing on biomimicry, with floating magnetic beds and plants that pump oxygen into the air while removing carbon dioxide. The first carbon-neutral hotel is already operating in Shanghai, and we expect more to come.

The 2010s will also bring focused exploration of the role of brands in a challenging business environment. We expect the number of brands to continue to grow even as PricewaterhouseCoopers lists over three hundred hotel brands competing for lodging dollars. At the same time, Internet distribution has become easier, enabling some hotels to distribute their product with no brand affiliation. Marriott has already grasped this concept, creating its Autograph Collection of independent hotels with access to Marriott's booking engine. This suggests that, in the 2010s, branding-related research will focus more on the distribution of products as part of brand viability. Simon Cooper, chief operating officer of Ritz-Carlton, was quoted as saying, "The customer is much less brand-conscious. They are looking beneath the brand, under the tag, and asking, 'Is this a good value for me?'—whether it is a handbag or a hotel."[21]

Another question is whether the hotel industry will follow the airlines by charging for everything possible. Hotels have always charged for rooms with a view and for certain services (phone calls, Internet access, in-room movies). However, all those services (and their attendant fees) are relatively easy to avoid. The question for the hotel industry is, Are there additional opportunities to charge for products previously included in the price? Other questions follow: At what point does add-on pricing become an irritant and drive business away? For instance, are there guests who avoid hotel chains that charge for Wi-Fi service? In other words, which products or amenities should be bundled? These considerations will drive industry prices in the 2010s.

We expect revenue management job descriptions in the coming decade to include maximizing profit, which is likely to make data convergence a key trend. We can imagine a reservation system that is able, for every customer, to integrate booking history, website surfing history, guest history, on-property feedback, folio information, comment card data, and satisfaction survey responses into an individual guest profile, enabling hotels to develop the best product and price offer possible for every guest.

Emerging new travel markets will represent another challenge and opportunity for hospitality marketers. By 2020, there will be as many as one hundred million Chinese and fifty million Indians traveling overseas even as domestic tourism in these two countries skyrockets. Adapting marketing strategies to this domestic and international travel volume will fuel long-term growth.

Finally, we expect marketers to become adept at using integrated data sets and novel analytical techniques. Hospitality marketers are beginning to realize that their primary focus should be on investing in profitable customer relationships. This will require, first, that we view marketing as an investment, not just an expense. Marketers must focus on estimating returns on every marketing dollar invested, using return on marketing investment (ROMI) as a key metric. Second, smart marketers will make profit per customer, not just revenue, the key goal. Third, customer relationships will continue to supplant customer transactions as a focal point; a key measure of these relationships is lifetime value. We expect that estimating the net present value of future cash flows from each customer or customer account will determine how much to invest in each relationship.

1 For most of this time, the journal was known as *Cornell Hotel and Restaurant Administration Quarterly*, but in this book we use the current nomenclature.

2 Later published as C. Dewitt Coffman, *Marketing for a Full House* (Ithaca, NY: Cornell Hotel and Restaurant Administration Quarterly, 1972).

3 David C. Dorf, "Package Plan Promotion," *Cornell Hotel and Restaurant Administration Quarterly* 2, no. 3 (1961): 51–54.

4 H. Victor Grohman, "Internal Promotion for Hotels," *Cornell Hotel and Restaurant Administration Quarterly* 2, no. 3 (1961): 29–35.

5 See Robert L. Bliss, "PLAN Your Public Relations Program: A Public Relations Counsel Outlines a Program of Successful Community Service for Hotel Men," *Cornell Hotel and Restaurant Administration Quarterly* 1, no. 3 (1960): 29–31; and Edward C. Bursk, "The Marketing Concept: A New Approach to Hotel Management; Alert Hosts in the Marketing Age," *Cornell Hotel and Restaurant Administration Quarterly* 7, no. 4 (1967): 2–8.

6 William Morton, "Closing the Marketing Gap," *Cornell Hotel and Restaurant Administration Quarterly* 7, no. 4 (1967): 9–16.

7 *Cornell Hotel and Restaurant Administration Quarterly,* "Reservation Systems: Communication Network That Sells the Rooms," *Cornell Hotel and Restaurant Administration Quarterly* 8, no. 4 (1968): 11–16.

8 Leven is currently president and chief operating officer of Las Vegas Sands. The quote is from Philip Kotler, John T. Bowen, and James Makens, *Marketing for Hospitality and Tourism,* 5th ed. (Upper Saddle River, NJ: Pearson Prentice Hall, 2009), 3.

9 See Graham Campbell-Smith, "Marketing the Meal Experience," *Cornell Hotel and Restaurant Administration Quarterly* 11, no. 1 (1970): 73–102; William R. Swinyard, "A Research Approach to Restaurant Marketing," *Cornell Hotel and Restaurant Administration Quarterly* 17, no. 4 (1977): 56–61; and Charles Ramond, "Advertising Research for the Food Service Industry," *Cornell Hotel and Restaurant Administration Quarterly* 18, no. 1 (1977): 20–32.

10 See Clarence H. Peters, "Pre-opening Market Analysis for Hotels," *Cornell Hospitality and Restaurant Administration Quarterly* 19, no. 1 (1978): 15–22; Peter C. Yesawich, "Post-opening Market Analysis for Hotels," *Cornell Hospitality and Restaurant Administration Quarterly* 19, no. 3 (1978): 70–81; and Peter C. Yesawich, "The Execution and Measurement of a Marketing Program," *Cornell Hospitality and Restaurant Administration Quarterly* 20, no. 1 (1979): 41–52.

11 Eric B. Orkin, "Boosting Your Bottom Line with Yield Management," *Cornell Hospitality and Restaurant Administration Quarterly* 28, no. 4 (1988): 52–56; Walter J. Relihan, "The Yield Management Approach to Hotel-Room Pricing," *Cornell Hospitality and Restaurant Administration Quarterly* 30, no. 1 (1989): 40–45; and Sheryl E. Kimes, "The Basics of Yield Management," *Cornell Hospitality and Restaurant Administration Quarterly* 30, no. 3 (1989): 14–19.

12 Kotler, Bowen, and Makens, *Marketing for Hospitality and Tourism,* 240.

13 John T. Bowen and Stowe Shoemaker, "Loyalty: A Strategic Commitment," *Cornell Hospitality and Restaurant Administration Quarterly* 39, no. 1 (1998): 12–23.

14 Laurette Dubé and Leo M. Renaghan, "Building Customer Loyalty: Guests' Perspectives on the Lodging Industry's Functional Best Practices," *Cornell Hospitality and Restaurant Administration Quarterly* 40, no. 5 (1999): 78–88.

15 Richard Labagh and Jonathan D. Barsky, "A Strategy for Customer Satisfaction," *Cornell Hospitality and Restaurant Administration Quarterly* 33, no. 5 (1992): 32–40; Laurette Dubé, Leo M. Renaghan, and Jane M. Miller, "Measuring Customer Satisfaction for Strategic Management," *Cornell Hospitality and Restaurant Administration Quarterly* 35, no. 1 (1994): 39–47; and Atila Yüksel and Mike Rimmington, "Customer-Satisfaction Measurement: Performance Counts," *Cornell Hospitality and Restaurant Administration Quarterly* 39, no. 6 (1998): 60–70.

16 Chekitan S. Dev and Ellis D. Bernard, "Guest Histories: An Untapped Service Resource," *Cornell Hospitality and Restaurant Administration Quarterly* 32, no. 2 (1991): 28.

17 Seymus Baloglu, "Dimensions of Customer Loyalty: Separating Friends from Well Wishers," *Cornell Hospitality and Restaurant Administration Quarterly* 43, no. 1 (2002): 47–59; Jonathan Barsky and Leonard Nash, "Evoking Emotion: Affective Keys to Hotel Loyalty," *Cornell Hotel and Restaurant Administration Quarterly* 43, no. 1 (2002): 39–46.

18 Peter O'Connor and Andrew J. Frew, "The Future of Hotel Electronic Distribution: Expert and Industry Perspectives," *Cornell Hotel and Restaurant Administration Quarterly* 43, no. 2 (2002): 33–45.

19 Roland Schegg, Susanne Frey, Jamie Murphy, and Doina Olaru, "Swiss Hotels' Web-site and E-mail Management: The Bandwagon Effect," *Cornell Hotel and Restaurant Administration Quarterly* 44, no. 1 (2003): 71–87.

20 Sunmee Choi and Sheryl Kimes, "Electronic Distribution Channels' Effect on Hotel Revenue Management," *Cornell Hotel and Restaurant Administration Quarterly* 43, no. 3 (2002): 23–31.

21 Joe Sharkey, "At High-End Hotels, Business Is Looking Up," *New York Times,* May 11, 2010, B6.

CHAPTER TWO

Branding Challenges and Opportunities

This chapter distills important lessons from an event that brought luminaries from industry and the academy together to discuss cutting-edge developments in branding, which is the central organizing principle for most hospitality organizations. The roundtable gathering outlined below addressed a host of brand-related issues, including global brand building, brand value, promoting brands over the Internet, legal rights, and design.

The Brand Roundtable

The Cornell Hospitality Brand Management Roundtable at the Center for Hospitality Research (CHR) at Cornell University was designed as a one-day, interactive, high-level discussion among a select group of thirty brand executives, consultants, and professors who shared their experience and knowledge on a variety of key brand management topics. The roundtable featured provocative presentations of cutting-edge research studies by leading scholars collaborating with industry partners. Each fifty-minute session kicked off with a twenty-minute presentation by "provocateurs" on each subject, leaving a full thirty minutes for discussion.

Building Successful Global Brands

The opening session provocateurs, Ed Lebar and Seth Traum of BrandAsset Consulting, explained how to transform customer data into effective brand strategy, especially given the "sea of sameness" that afflicts many brands. Lebar and Traum identified four pillars of brand development from the BrandAsset Valuator model of brand equity: *energized differentiation, relevance, esteem,* and *knowledge.* These pillars stand on brand strength and brand stature. A brand begins by building energized differentiation and achieves relevance as it enters consumer consideration sets. Eventually, the brand is esteemed by its patrons, some of whom become truly loyal. Some consumers become deeply knowledgeable about the brand and turn into brand evangelists. All this begins with energized differentiation and relevance because, in the lodging category, energized differentiation is highly correlated with revenue per available room (RevPAR) and average daily room rate (ADR), and relevance is related to occupancy rate.

Brands typically experience a life cycle that extends beyond the differentiation-and-growth phase. Lebar and Traum used brand strength and brand stature to construct a matrix capturing a brand's life cycle position in relation to other brands. On the resulting matrix, called a "PowerGrid," brands fall into either the undeveloped quadrant, the niche quadrant, the commoditized quadrant, or the leadership quadrant. A brand with both high strength and high stature is a leadership brand that enjoys customer commitment. In other cases, many brands that have developed high brand stature but lack brand strength are commodity brands, which can work relatively well for low-cost, high-volume operations. By contrast, a luxury brand needs high brand strength to maintain its niche positioning. The key is aligning a brand's strategy with its position. For example, W Hotels has developed into a strong niche brand, although it is not a high-volume brand. Very few lodging brands fall into the leadership quadrant with high brand strength and brand stature, even when evaluated by frequent travelers.

The typical brand life cycle settles into the commodity quadrant, often through diminished energized differentiation. Traum explained that a brand can escape this fate by focusing on building brand strength through a combination of new product development and effective branding and marketing. Within its category, for example, Holiday Inn has worked to move in the leadership direction by adding new properties and removing old ones.

Extending the brand life cycle is especially difficult in the hospitality industry because the various traveler segments seek dissimilar brand characteristics. Frequent-travelers' perceptions of hospitality brands are, for example, more sharply defined than are those of leisure travelers, reflecting highly specific points of differentiation in prestige, distinctiveness, and upper-class ambiance. Global brands must achieve and maintain consistency, according to Lebar, representing the same message in every market. Even a powerful brand will have trouble sustaining growth with a different image in every country. Consistent global branding also creates efficiencies that relieve brand managers of the burden of determining the brand's position for each country. Because a brand essentially promises a set of benefits, it is essential to build trust into the brand message. A brand that lacks trust and integrity will not survive. Finally, global branding depends on developing a community of like-minded people. The right combination of efficiency, trust, and community leads to superior financial performance.

Branding by Amenity

The lodging industry's well-known trend of "amenity creep" is often attributed to brands' efforts to differentiate themselves. Most industry operators would agree, however, that the expense involved in adding amenities has not always created the hoped-for differentiation. Seeking to unravel the amenities equation, Starwood collaborated with professors at Cornell (Chekitan Dev) and the University of Maryland (Rebecca Hamilton and Roland Rust) to conduct a systematic study of amenities that guests actually want and use. In particular, the study sought a way to calculate return on the amenities investment, dubbed ROA (return on amenities). Matt Valenti and Jennifer Sabet of Starwood joined Professor Hamilton for the presentation.

Professor Hamilton explained that hotel guests, like other consumers, often fail to use amenities they predict they'll use. Before using products, that is, consumers tend to focus on desirability (why they want the products); after using products, however, they tend to focus on usability (how they actually used the product). For this study, *amenities* covered a wide range of services and features, including valet parking, kiosk check-in, guest room television and desk chair, a hair drier, and a safe. The research team was interested in whether hotel guests would experience a similar "flip-flop" in their amenity preferences before and after their hotel stays. In a word, the answer is yes: as expected, the survey found that predicted amenity use was generally higher than actual amenity use. The study also found that charging for amenities affected amenity use and satisfaction. Usage charges increased the gap between predicted and actual use of amenities, although the reaction to such charges varied across market segments.

Calculation of return on amenities must take into account the extent to which a guest's decision to stay is based on predicted amenity use and actual amenity use. As Valenti pointed out, however, guests who used more amenities were significantly more satisfied with their stays and were therefore more likely to return. However, brand managers must also understand systematic mispredictions of amenity use, Professor Hamilton concluded, because decisions to stay at a property may be based more on what guests think they will use than on what they actually use.

Brand Value

In search of ways to unlock the value of their lodging assets, hotel owners have, according to STR Global, changed the names of twelve thousand hotels in the past three decades. The reflagging curve has gone exponential. The question is, What financial outcomes result from reflagging a property? A joint proprietary study by Cornell, the University of Chicago, and PKF Hospitality Research (PKF-HR) identified three ways in which hotels reflag: brand-to-brand, independent-to-brand, and brand-to-independent. The study captured profit and loss data for two years prior to the rebranding, during the rebranding year, and for two years following, matching the hotels to a control group that did not rebrand but are located in the same metropolitan areas. Although balance sheet information was not available, the two groups were compared for increases in occupancy rate, ADR, RevPAR, rooms revenue, total revenues, marketing expenses, gross operating profit (GOP), and net operating income (NOI).

Researchers Mark Woodworth, president of PKF-HR, and Cornell's Chekitan Dev reported that after rebranding, the test group saw increases in ADR, RevPAR, and revenues, but also a substantial increase in marketing expense. These differences were significant. Considering just the brand-to-brand conversions, RevPAR increased by 12 percent. However, when comparison is made with the control group, the increase says more about occupancy, resulting in only a 5 percent RevPAR lift that can be attributed to the brand changeover.

Hotels undergoing brand-to-independent conversions saw drops in occupancy, but they still recorded an 11 percent increase in RevPAR. Compared with their control group, however, although the newly independent properties had increased ADR, there was no other identifiable benefit beyond a drop in marketing expenses. Conversely, these hotels experienced, on average, a 35 percent decline in NOI.

Properties undergoing independent-to-brand conversions enjoyed increases in occupancy, ADR, and (thus) RevPAR, but they also experienced considerable increases in marketing expenses. These greater marketing costs offset the identified revenue gains, resulting in slight declines in NOI.

These data allowed Woodworth and Dev to break out the effects of specific brands on reflagging. Some brands added more value than they extracted from a property, but others absorbed value. Thus, because of drops in occupancy, certain brands are significantly negative in RevPAR. Most brands increased ADR, but not all increased occupancy, and the change in total revenue was not always favorable.

These results notwithstanding, Woodworth cautioned that having a brand is typically critical to securing financing for a project. In a recent meeting with fifty lenders, he found that all of them preferred a flag, while only a select few would fund an independent property. Thus, even if a brand technically extracted more value than it contributed, if there would have been no deal without it, the brand undeniably brought value to the owner.

Noting the critical matter of brand expenses, Ted Teng of Leading Hotels recalled the reflagging policy when he was with Wyndham. He pointed out that the chain always rebranded its owned hotels to Wyndham whenever possible, even if there was a rate or occupancy hit, because that allowed the chain to capture marketing and brand expenses instead of paying them to another flag.

BRANDING IN THE INTERNET AGE

Paul Brown of Hilton Worldwide shared Hilton's approach to engaging consumers in its brands through online channels. The new model is completely topsy-turvy, he said, since the original idea of a web search involved a top-down approach, as people would go to a site and gradually drill down to discover the inventory. Now it's sideways navigation at best, and the average traveler can visit as many as twenty-two websites before booking. As a result, Hilton changed its focus on channel management to evaluate the activities of the online teams, hoping to influence the decision process and maximize retail presence. It's about more than just securing one booking.

Borrowing a phrase from product marketers, Brown said that "shelf space" is an essential consideration—that is, having the brand appear, under Hilton's retail guidelines, in as many relevant locations as possible as many times as possible. That is, in addition to building great brands that deliver relevant product and experience and send a proper message, a brand must ensure appropriate product distribution along all relevant channels. In this way, a brand can demonstrate its value to owners in part by showing its shelf space on the global distribution system (GDS), on web-based business-to-consumer channels, or in sales relationships.

Brown noted that there's "lots of noise" regarding online travel agents (OTAs) in the lodging industry, but the OTAs matter mostly because of the transparency they provide. If a brand is in fact an undifferentiated commodity or perceived as one of low quality or service, this becomes readily apparent to consumers as they search on the web. This underscores the importance of effective differentiation and proper alignment of the product with the channel. Brown agrees that the economics of OTAs appear troubling, but argues that they have a billboard effect and in many cases open up incremental segments. That said, OTA costs are expected to continue to decrease over time as alternative distribution channels emerge and direct online channels become even more effective.

According to Brown, Hilton tries to maintain visibility and ease of navigation across all core retail and search channels. It's essential to establish consistent product pricing across all channels and to provide the customer with compelling reasons to use direct channels as much as possible. The use of direct channels increases yield, as does encouraging guests to participate in a loyalty program. Customers who are members of Hilton HHonors, for example, are two to three times more likely to book through direct channels.

To achieve a holistic view of a channel, in this case OTAs, brand managers must weigh the pros and cons. The pros for OTAs: they provide value through being on the shelf, including the billboard effect; they reach a distinctive customer base; they offer relatively compelling yield if well managed; their contract rules can set terms and price stability; and the channel returns relatively high ROI on promotions and marketing. The cons: OTAs are relatively expensive and bid up the cost of search terms; they generally offer lower reported ADRs and relatively inflexible inventory controls; and, most critically from a brand management point of view, the brand does not have a direct connection with the consumer when booking occurs.

The Brand as a Bundle of Rights

Longtime hospitality litigator Jim Renard of the law firm of Bickel Brewer brought the roundtable up to speed on issues relating to brands and the law. To Renard a brand is in large part a bundle of intellectual property rights: service marks, copyrighted materials, and trade secrets. Companies that own all their hotels face few legal challenges in terms of acquiring marks and copyrights and keeping trade secrets.

Challenges arise, however, in connection with third-party management agreements and franchise contracts, pursuant to which brand owners (i.e., chains) convey to others the right to use or to affiliate hotels with their brands. Among the most contentious provisions in management contracts are protection clauses—a major breeding ground for brand-related disputes—by which hotel owners are effectively given enforceable rights against the brand owners themselves. Further contributing to such controversies is the fundamental legal principle that the operator is an agent of the hotel owner and owes the owner fiduciary duties, even if the contract disavows that relationship.

Recent, ongoing industry consolidation has increased the number of territory disputes. In some instances, mergers and acquisitions have led to unintended encroachments. In addition, the proliferation of "co-brands" and "endorsed" brands has given rise to numerous claims of breaches of restrictive covenants and territorial exclusivity clauses. Renard explained that many such disputes arise because of poorly crafted contract language as well as the failure on the part of some management companies and franchisors to monitor and coordinate their development activities within the limitations and restrictions imposed on them by existing contracts with third-party owners. Renard urged all brand purveyors to be aware of the provisions of their contracts and to ensure compliance with their obligations as they build brand value.

BRANDING BY DESIGN

Several roundtable discussions acknowledged that design is a critical aspect of any brand's positioning. Howard Wolff of WATG illustrated how branding by design is part art and part science. The science comes from understanding the elements of good design. As Wolff explained them, they are *functionality, quality,* and *impact.* More specifically, excellent design fulfills its purpose, is built to last, and lifts people's spirits.

Taking those principles as a basis, Wolff referenced a tool called DQI (Design Quality Indicator) to quantify how design adds value to a project. Hyatt tested it on thirty of their owned hotels and was able to correlate the DQI scores with guest and employee satisfaction as well as with the hotels' RevPAR index. WATG has also examined the effect of design on a property's top and bottom lines and found that WATG hotels that embody its design principles outperformed the control group in occupancy, ADR, and RevPAR.

Wolff argued that effective design adds asset value even as it reduces operating and maintenance costs, improves productivity and the guest experience, and builds brand identity through recognition, visibility, and media exposure. Wolff cautioned that a brand is defined by its customers. Good design emphasizes and reflects the brand's promises.

While it's easy to think of guest satisfaction on a single continuum, Wolff sees two linear scales of customer satisfaction. Along the first one, if you fix something that's wrong you can turn a dissatisfied customer into a satisfied guest. The second scale starts with a satisfied customer and creates a guest who loves the property. Design, as Wolff illustrated with examples, can help to move guests into the "love it" category.

Wolff also recommended asking employees to discover the design issues that a property faces. Guests come and go, but employees deal with a property's design weaknesses every day. Based on research conducted by Wolff, the top complaints cited by employees about a hotel's design are also noted by guests: insufficient lighting, inadequate work spaces, poor temperature control, slow elevators, confusing navigation (poor signage), and maintenance issues. As Wolff sees it, you can't have a great hotel if your employees don't like the place. There is also a bottom line benefit to having happy employees that can be measured in terms of productivity, morale, turnover…and guest satisfaction.

Finally, Wolff cited another study, according to which, to get the most bang for the buck when renovating, a property should redo the lobby before the guest rooms. Still, renovating guest rooms and the lobby together had an even greater impact on guest satisfaction and ROI. At resort properties, investing in landscaping and enhancing the arrival experience can also generate handsome returns.

Conclusion

The goal of the first CHR Brand Management Roundtable was to provoke change and push the status quo. The global-brandscape discussion defined the trends to which global brand leaders need to pay more attention. The brand amenities discussion identified the key amenities that drive usage and satisfaction. The brand value discussion defined a new and better way for brands to track their competitive performance as they contemplate reflagging. The branding-in-the-Internet-age keynote provocation led to new perspectives on the future of brands online, including how hotel brands and OTAs can better live together. The brand rights discussion determined how brand rights should be established in management agreements. The branding-by-design discussion focused on aspects of design that drive guest engagement. In summary, this roundtable provided attendees an opportunity to showcase their thought leadership, to offer insights, and to learn from some spirited and informative discussions that forged new understandings across the industry-academy divide.

CHAPTER THREE

Branding and the Internet

Today, the dominant Internet usage paradigm is Web 2.0, featuring interactive applications that are context sensitive to user-generated data and social relationships. Users carry smart phones and tablet computers, searching out information to make real-time purchases and reservations. A relatively recent outgrowth of the resulting time compression in marketing and sales is the phenomenon of *social couponing,* offered through *daily deals, flash sales,* and *private sales.* In 2010, e-commerce in the United States generated $228 billion in sales, including $85 billion for travel services, which grew by 73 percent from 2005 through 2010.[1] Flash sale sites have helped fuel this growth in e-commerce.

The Challenge

The hospitality industry is not sure what to make of these new marketing channels, which seem capable of generating new business and even boosting profits. The novelty of the social couponing business model may, however, discourage some brands from risking their image on steep discounts. To understand the risks and benefits involved in flash sales and daily deals, research must explore this segment of the e-commerce environment. This chapter focuses on the use of flash sale and daily deal sites in the hospitality industry, reporting a study based on a survey of relevant practices in the global hotel industry that examines flash sales strategies and approaches. The chapter concludes by pinpointing opportunities and identifying challenges associated with these emerging marketing and branding channels.

FLASH SALES: DAILY DEALS VERSUS PRIVATE SALES

The study divided flash sales into daily deal sites, such as Groupon and LivingSocial, and private sales sites, led by Gilt Groupe, Rue La La, HauteLook, and Ideeli. Flash sales typically offer customers promotions of short duration that provide dramatic savings—usually contingent on achieving a threshold of customers accepting the proposed deal. When a deal goes live on a flash sale website, past customers and e-mail subscribers receive e-mail notification, and many flash sale sites also promote deals via social networking sites. In contrast, the marketing and branding strategy behind private sales sites assumes that requiring consumers to register for membership creates a perception of exclusivity that prevents deep discounts from harming the brands. Instead, brands are promoted by targeting a select subset of consumers, for a short time, presumably thereby strengthening consumer-brand relationships.

Since 2008, the phenomenal popularity of flash deals has made them appealing marketing and branding channels for restaurants, hotels, and resorts. Despite concerns about cannibalizing existing demand, the exposure that hospitality brands enjoy through intermediaries is thought to help bring in new customers, increase sales, increase brand recognition, and encourage repeat business. The catch is that these intermediaries are able to charge significant commissions (ranging from 20 to 50 percent) on top of requesting significant discounts in the nominal value-to-price ratio of the items sold (50 percent and up). This study undertook a systematic evaluation of the benefits and drawbacks of these channels.

THE FLASH SALE HOSPITALITY MARKET

Daily Deal Travel Websites. Most daily deals websites are opportunistic, offering a variety of goods and services, including travel. In August 2011 travel deals were the third largest category of daily deals. Even though travel offers accounted for only 3 percent of the total number of deals, the travel and tourism category yielded the highest revenue per deal.

That revenue potential has attracted considerable interest. For example, Priceline has been testing local deals for spas, restaurants, and retail offers and Travelocity has launched "Dashing Deals," which can be booked directly instead of requiring redemption of a coupon or voucher for future travel. Perhaps the most interesting development so far is the Groupon-Expedia partnership, which with "Groupon Getaways" competes directly with LivingSocial Escapes, LivingSocial's travel deals product. In its first full month of operations, according to Yipit, Groupon Getaways outperformed LivingSocial Escapes, generating 42 percent more revenue than LivingSocial Escapes did and averaging 78 percent higher revenue per deal.[2]

Private Sales Travel Websites. On private sales sites, customers sign up for or "enroll" in a program, usually with no fee or payment required, and receive regular e-mail notices about time-limited discount offers and promotions. Private sales sector actors fall roughly into three categories: travel-only sites; retail-oriented sites that include a travel component in their offer, often through partnership with travel specialists; and online travel agent sites that have added "private sales" to their websites.

To increase membership, most sites offer credits for referrals that lead to purchases, which can be used on future bookings, and unique amenities or features. Discounts from advertised rates on private sale sites are usually around 30 percent, but occasionally run much higher. The purchase window is typically no longer than a week. Some sites seek differentiation by adopting a slightly different model.

Most sites offer firm reservations for fixed dates and vouchers that remain valid over a period of several months, subject to availability, which usually involves midweek dates—which means that not all consumers can use their vouchers. It is costly for consumers to renege on private sale deals, since most are either nonrefundable or carry large cancellation penalties.[3]

MARKET TRENDS IN TRAVEL FLASH SALES

The core market involves travel sites that offer enticing discounts at top-end properties, which are seeking to fill rooms when occupancy rates are low. These sites appeal to a growing segment that skews toward women and the well educated with above-average incomes. While some customers may find discounts for previously planned trips, others are seeking travel arrangements and accommodations for specific destinations, and a few have sufficient time and cash at their disposal for impromptu vacations.

The market is also beginning to accommodate customers in the midscale range, distinguishing themselves with a focus on another set of target demographics as they jockey for customer loyalty. For example, LivingSocialEscapes now offers trips for people who prefer to stay close to home, offering deals that include day trips and weekend jaunts with no air travel. Midscale consumers like these deals because they make trip planning easy.

Business models continue to multiply. Yuupon targets customers with both modest and high-end offers. Their users are not required to choose travel dates at time of purchase, refunds are available until the day before travel, there is no group minimum required for a deal to go live, offers last for seven days, and all vacations are fully transferable. Jetsetter offers discounted travel deals without flash sales, to appeal to consumers who do not enjoy the time pressure or group connection. However, Jetsetter generally features exotic or unique locales, which may not be a realistic option for many consumers. It appears that hotel chains are also testing flash deals, such as an "exclusive" offer from Accor Hotels, valid for forty-eight hours. Clearly, the major hotel companies have realized the value of this type of marketing initiative.

The Study

The survey sample was drawn from the global subscriber base of the Cornell Center for Hospitality Research. Although 225 respondents started the survey and only 136 answered all the questions, the respondents constituted a fairly well distributed global sample representing five continents. Regarding usage, there was a generally even split between those who had used flash sale sites (42%) and those who had not considered using such channels (46%). The remaining 12 percent of the respondents were considering usage.

Respondent job functions were quite diverse, with almost half coming from a combination of sales and marketing (28%), revenue management (13%), and distribution (3%). A quarter of the respondents held general management (20%) or executive positions (6%), with the balance comprising professionals in almost all other areas of hotel management. The bulk of respondents worked on-property, with far fewer corporate and regional office respondents. The sample was widely distributed in both property location and star rating, with a majority of the hotels located in urban areas (60%), several in small metro areas (16%) and suburban areas (16%), and the rest near airports or highways. In terms of star ratings or price point, the sample was widely distributed among upper midscale (23%), luxury (19%), upper upscale (17%), upscale (16%), and midscale (16%), with the rest in the economy or bed-and-breakfast segments.

Results

FLASH SALE AND PRIVATE SALE SITES USED

Each of the forty-six operators who had used flash deals cited at least one recently launched deal. This approach yielded a sample of sixty-nine deals and promotions offered on twenty-three intermediaries globally. Groupon and LivingSocial were the most popular sites in our sample (cited by 31% and 14%, respectively), with Jetsetter emerging as the most popular private sale site (10%). Rue La La, Vacationist, HauteLook, and Travelzoo trailed, with none cited by more than 7 percent of respondents.

Usage Profile

Many respondents were heavy users of flash sales, with an average of four-teen promotions per property to date. Even after deleting heavy users from the sample we found that the deals were fairly popular, as the remaining respondents had run an average of about three flash and private sales.

The promotions reported by heavy users tended to be for short stays—an average of about two nights per promotion, with one-night stays comprising 35 percent, two-night stays 30 percent, and three-night stays about 21 percent. The most common discount percentage (42% of all deals) was between 45 and 55 percent. There was a wide range of discounts, however, with some as little as 15 percent and some over 75 percent.

More commissions paid to intermediaries fell into the 15- to 20-percent range than any other, and 50 percent of commissions were lower than 20 percent. This belies the widespread notion that all flash sale intermediaries charge 50 percent commissions. Nevertheless, fully one-fifth of the deals ran with commissions of over 40 percent.

Comparing Users and Nonusers

There was little difference by size and location between users and nonusers of flash sale sites. There were, however, some differences between users and nonusers with respect to property type and location. About 53 percent of upscale properties had used flash deals, as had 45 percent of upper up-scale hotels and 41 percent of luxury properties. The other property types were as follows: bed and breakfast, about 28 percent users versus 56 percent nonusers; economy, 38 percent users versus 38 percent nonusers; and mid-scale, 39 percent users versus 52 percent nonusers. In terms of location, users outnumbered nonusers only in suburban locations (48% to 28%), with 39 percent of urban properties, 32 percent of highway properties, 28 percent of small metro properties, and 27 percent of airport properties reporting having tested a flash deal.

These results should be interpreted with caution, given the low number of respondents in each subgroup, but it appears that hotels with more services have greater potential to take advantage of flash sales because of their superior ability to bundle those services and offset steep room discounts tempered by ancillary revenue. Hotels that used flash sale sites offered on average 2.57 ser-vices beyond accommodation, compared with 1.72 for nonusers. Deal users were also more likely to offer restaurants, spas, casinos, convention facilities, excursions, and golf courses.

Performance pressure may also play a role in flash sales, with about 23 percent of users reporting that they felt such pressure versus 12 percent who were nonusers.

Reasons for Offering Flash Deals

When picking from six possible reasons for running each of the promotions they offered, respondents identified branding and customer acquisition most often, followed by profits and revenue optimization. Perhaps this was because 28 percent of the respondents were sales and marketing executives versus 13 percent who were involved in revenue management. Respondents indicated that they rarely engaged in flash or private sale deals out of desperation, suggesting that the majority of operators are choosing these intermediaries with some deliberation.

The purpose of a deal was cross-referenced with each of the most popular intermediaries. Travelzoo was used most often to boost occupancy, while Vacationist was the most popular choice for boosting profitability.

Usage Strategies

Regarding how brands ensure maximum ROI from flash sales sites, their responses exhibited a wide variety of approaches, starting with capacity constraints. Respondents said that they used LivingSocial for the widest array of strategies, especially to ensure separation of an offer's perceived value and its actual cost. This site also allowed hotels to encourage customers to upgrade and purchase incremental services as well as systematically encourage customer loyalty. On the other hand, capacity constraints were invoked most often with Travelzoo.

Additional insights were related to the degree of sophistication of the operators engaging in flash sale promotions. The data suggest that Groupon users tend to limit revenue-maximizing strategies, perhaps relying on exposure and sheer numbers, whereas HauteLook and Travelzoo users aggressively employ a variety of strategies.

Satisfaction with Deal Promotions

Respondents were relatively satisfied with their promotions, but not all were enthusiastic and there was a lurking resistance to repeating deals. Two out of three deals were rated as at least somewhat successful, and about a quarter of the deals were rated as clearly successful. Only 5 percent were rated very disappointing, suggesting that this marketing channel is not going away anytime soon. Intentions to try another promotion were fairly high, and 65 percent of respondents were willing to recommend the intermediary they used. Even so, when asked whether they would run the same promotions, only about half of our respondents said they strongly or mildly agreed, and 29 percent were strongly negative about particular deals. Given the chance to change their offers, 68 percent were at least slightly likely to try again.

Respondents agreed with one of the most frequently touted benefits of flash sale promotions: exposure to new customers. On average respondents reported hosting 70 percent new customers through their flash and private sale promotions. Yet the findings did not support one of the great concerns with flash sale sites, which is that they attract bargain hunters.

On the other hand, flash sale promotion seems not to generate repeat business. Respondents reported that an average of only 11 percent of customers returned from each promotion. The highest percentage of repeat business came from Vacationist, at 16 percent. Repeat-business percentages from other sites were 15 percent for Rue La La, 13 percent for Groupon, 5.5 percent for Living-Social, and 5 percent for Jetsetter.

CORRELATES OF SATISFACTION, REPEAT USAGE, AND REFERRALS

The data showed a statistically significant correlation between satisfaction with a promotion and the percentage of new customers the promotion attracted, but a weaker correlation between satisfaction and customers' excess spending. In other words, operators perceived initiatives to be successful when they broadened the customer base, even if the new customers failed to spend significantly more during their stay.

Those results were corroborated by whether the respondent would recommend the site to others. A significant correlation emerged between the likelihood of recommending a site and the percentage of new customers the promotion attracted. There was no significant correlation of recommendations with on-property spending.

With respect to the strategy implemented, there was a significant correlation only between management of the total cost of a promotion by hotel brands and perceived satisfaction. In other words, those who reported paying more attention to managing the total cost of a promotion were significantly more satisfied than were those who did not do so. No other strategy correlated strongly with satisfaction.

This strategy of managing the total cost of a promotion also was correlated with a higher likelihood of recommending a site. Moreover, a positive view of an intermediary was strongly correlated with proactive management of the loyalty of newly attracted guests. Weaker, but positive, correlations were detected with proactive management of variable costs, the cross-selling of services to increase incremental sales, and the implementation of capacity constraints to avoid displacement of higher-margin business.

WHY RESPONDENTS AVOIDED FLASH DEALS

The reasons given by respondents who would not consider flash sales coalesced around the following themes.

- Expense: channels insist on too steep a discount and too high a commission.
- Misalignment with target customer segment: emphasized by the luxury segment.
- Negative branding effects: undermining rate integrity and future expectations.
- Ignorance: lack of familiarity with these channels.

Given the importance of rate integrity and brand expectations, we asked those who had used flash deals to comment on whether they thought the sales they had offered compromised rate integrity. The results were intriguing. Three out of four generally believed that rate integrity was not compromised, but only one out of four stated that they were sure of this assessment.

PROSPECTIVE USERS

Finally, we asked the small group of respondents who were still considering the use of flash sales and private sales to state the factors that would push them to take this step. About 40 percent cited the hope of increasing occupancy rates, 38 percent cited customer acquisition, 37 percent cited brand management, 34 percent cited revenue enhancement, 33 percent cited boosting profit, and 26 percent said they would do it out of desperation.

Actionable Insights

On balance, the study found that hotel brands that used flash sales did well. To brands that hope to improve their use of flash sales and those still considering it, the following recommendations were offered.

- Define your purpose: pick the right site for the right reasons.
- Study sites carefully: understand the business model.

- Accept market insights from site representatives.
- Negotiate: terms vary and some sites are willing.
- Manage cost structure: calculate profit, volume, and ancillary revenue.
- Calculate room-nights needed and determine the best available times.
- Employ unique package deals to avoid cannibalization and protect market position.
- Start small; then adjust.
- Monitor user profiles and usage continually.
- Have a strategy for converting first-time users to repeaters; encourage referrals.

To maximize the benefits of flash or private sales, brands should balance repurchase potential against margin potential. Evaluating a property on these two dimensions better frames the value proposition offered by such deals. Brands that are unable to convert customers from flash sales deals into returning guests must manage deal margins carefully and pursue cross-selling and up-selling opportunities to on-property guests.

---

1 Gian Fulgoni [executive chair and cofounder, comScore Inc.], "Monetizing the Internet through Sales and Advertising" (PowerPoint presentation, Chicago Digital Collective Summit, Chicago, April 2011).

2 "Daily Deal Trends in North America," *Yipit Data Report,* August 12, 2011, http://www.digitaltrends.com/web/despite-downward-trend-groupon-revenue-grew-13-percent-in-august/ (accessed September 26, 2011).

3 Ed Perkins, "How to Navigate Travel Flash Sale Sites," *USA Today Travel,* August 24, 2011, http://travel.usatoday.com/deals/inside/story/2011–08–25/How-to-navigate-travel-flash-sale-sites/50125442/1 (accessed September 5, 2011).

Carnival Cruise Lines

arnival Cruise Lines is the market leader in the low-priced cruise market. Carnival achieved this position during a period of rapid growth in the industry by emphasizing onboard activities, targeting younger cruisers, using extensive television advertising, and focusing on the travel agent as its channel of distribution. With continuing industry growth, new companies are entering the business and existing liners are adding ships. Currently, Carnival controls 24 percent of the berth space in the North American market. Management must now decide how Carnival should burnish its brand in preparing for the future. In this commentary, I reflect on a case analysis presented by Professor Robert Kwortnik of Cornell University and offer some additional opportunities that Carnival might consider for further analytical exploration.[1]

Commentary

Professor Kwortnik introduces us to Carnival Cruise Lines as the dominant player in the entry-level cruise business with a brief history of the brand. He tells us that Carnival has enjoyed a string of successful and profitable years as a result of its unconventional marketing strategies. This has inspired many copy-cats who want to catch the wave of success in the cruise industry. Since Carnival's founding, the cruise industry has become fiercely competitive because of increased capacity, price discounting, and a "sea of sameness" that has all the cruise brands looking and sounding alike. Professor Kwortnik ends the section on the brand's evolution by opining that Carnival now faces the challenge of deciding how to best to burnish its brand for the future.

The analysis focuses on lack of brand differentiation, brand positioning, and brand equity and suggests the following strategies for improvement: define the brand's target market, identify brand purchase drivers, and define the brand's attributes. In closing his analysis Professor Kwortnik offers a retail analogy, suggesting that Carnival move up from being the Kmart to being the Walmart of the high seas. In the following sections, I reflect on the scope and strength of this analysis.

Overall, I felt the case was well presented and analyzed. Key points pertaining to the survival and success of the Carnival brand were highlighted and discussed. I agree with many of the suggestions Professor Kwortnik offers in his report. Particular strengths of his brand audit are the reexamination of Carnival's brand positioning and his questioning the continued relevance of its key brand attributes. Because he had done an excellent job of covering his bases, my contribution here is to offer supplemental brand strategies based on possible sources of additional threats to Carnival.

In particular, Professor Kwortnik's analysis could be expanded to include brand environment. Brand environment issues typically include challenges relating to product category, industry, and economy-level factors that can determine a brand's survival and success. In the following sections, I define these areas and reveal emerging opportunities.

What Might Keep Carnival Brand Stewards Awake at Night

In my opinion, this brand needs more than a little spit and polish; it needs to be seriously tinkered with if it is going to survive and succeed in the years ahead. Below I explain why the problem may be more severe than it appears.

SUBSTITUTE PRODUCTS

Many existing products in the hospitality and service fields are potential substitute products for a cruise. These products include hotels, destination resorts, all-inclusive resorts, time-shares, rental homes, air travel, trains, and casinos. Although none of these products supplies an experience that is identical to cruising, some could be combined to provide packages with similar features. Other potential substitute products—albeit unrelated to service or hospitality but nevertheless competing for the customer's disposable dollar—include discretionary expenditures on luxury items such as cars, furs, and jewels.

Substitute products play a fairly strong role in the cruise industry for several reasons. First, there is the problem of the perceived high cost of cruising that makes other options seem more reasonably priced. However, if all costs of a land-based vacation are totaled and compared with the price of a cruise, the cost typically is extremely close. Second, there are high switching costs because of the perceived high cost of a cruise experience and the fact that vacations may be a once-a-year option. Thus, other products on the market appear to be less risky purchases. Carnival's marketing department has determined that the primary purchase decision is whether to spend money on cruising or on luxury items. These substitutes represent real threats to the future of cruising.

BUYERS

Cruise buyers fall into two categories. The first is that of travel agents. Travel agents represent the primary distribution channel for Carnival. Consequently, travel agencies and agents are extremely important and powerful. Their influence matters at the point at which they recommend a Carnival cruise, a cruise on another line, or another type of vacation. If travel agents are the primary brand representatives for Carnival, any weakening of the brand risks confusion in the marketplace. Moreover, if travel agents were to band together, they could force a cruise line to reduce margins and pay higher commissions. Indeed, travel agents (e.g., Virtuoso) have organized to some degree, which increases their bargaining power.

The second category of buyers is that of the end user (the passenger). Because of the transparency offered by the Internet, passengers have become better educated about cruise offerings and can shop for attractive prices. Consequently, they have some power, but probably not enough to have a long-range impact on the industry. While the power of direct purchasers is therefore currently limited because they are small in number and fragmented, there is a real possibility that a stronger buyer group could depress prices and diminish Carnival's stellar profitability record.

POTENTIAL NEW ENTRANTS

The inability to fend off newer, more nimble, and unconventional competitive brands could torpedo Carnival's growth. With the outstanding success of the industry over the past ten years, many new entrants have begun or plan to begin operations. One recent entrant, EasyCruise, has positioned itself exactly where Carnival was at its inception: as *the* low cost provider. While EasyCruise is operating mainly in the Mediterranean, it could easily become a force to reckon with in North America. Every new entry into the cruise industry has some impact on Carnival.

However, the ability of any company to enter the market and have a sizable effect on Carnival's market share is limited. The cost of new ship construction has risen dramatically. Also, Carnival has a tremendous advantage in size that generates economies of scale. These economies allow Carnival to profit in the present market while being the lowest-priced competitor. Finally, Carnival has the advantage of being further along on the learning curve. So, while Carnival is in the crow's nest for now, this could change as new players disrupt the market.

Suppliers of Key Inputs

The supply that is paramount to cruise lines is air transportation. Airlines thus have the ability to negatively affect the cruise industry, and strikes or interruptions of service consequently have direct bottom-line impact. Additionally, the price that is charged for air tickets has a potentially major impact on a cruise line's ability to operate profitably. Recent rises in fuel prices and demand for oil from China and India promise to keep oil prices high for the foreseeable future. This could affect the economics of the cruise business dramatically.

Rivalry among Firms

Rivalry has intensified greatly in the cruise industry because of a sharp increase in berth space and the abovementioned blurring of distinctions across cruise brands. I found this trend captured almost perfectly in the Carnival brand campaign that featured the song "Beyond the Sea," with visuals that could represent any cruise line brand. I must admit, though, that I found myself humming the theme after watching the ad. So, while I might have objections on intellectual grounds about the song's capacity to adequately differentiate the brand, it hit this aging baby boomer on an emotional level and in that sense also hit its mark! Nevertheless, Carnival faces the challenge of deciding how best to position and differentiate its brand competitively to succeed in the future while avoiding a price and amenity war, as differentiation among brands continues to blur. Still, there are opportunities for Carnival to strengthen its brand, which I consider in the next section.

A Brand Manifesto for Carnival: Eleven Uneasy Pieces

In supplementing Professor Kwortnik's recommendations, I offer below eleven initiatives Carnival should consider in order to strengthen its brand.

1. As Professor Kwortnik suggests, there is an opportunity for Carnival to reconfigure its brand mantra. With its dominant market share, Carnival should

strive to move beyond its position as the lowest-cost provider to becoming the primary choice for the value-conscious passenger. Additional value-added services (e.g., premium wine sales, extended shore excursions, expanded spa services) would increase onboard revenues, thereby reducing the need to carry the greatest number of passengers. While this might seem to be an exercise in semantics, there is a real opportunity to carefully define brand value drivers and craft an optimum bundle of attributes.

2. Carnival needs to develop a strong relationship with the airlines that serve its ports. This would ensure its supply of discounted tickets and continue passenger transportation without interruption. Carnival might even consider co-branding with a specific airline as a preferred partner. A yet more radical option might be to enter the airline business itself or, as Virgin is doing, transport customers from their homes to the ship no matter where they live.

3. Given its high occupancy figures, a program of price increases might be feasible if Carnival were to use revenue management more aggressively. By focusing on profit per passenger, Carnival could balance the advantage of increased profit margins against the disadvantage of fewer passengers.

4. Carnival should consider expanding its brand into other niches. Offering Carnival-branded land-based resorts would give customers another option. By focusing on "customer equity," which is the value of its customer base, Carnival could create a powerful new revenue stream. If only 16 percent of Americans have taken a cruise, a substantial part of the other 84 percent have surely experienced a resort and represent a huge market for Carnival. While in pursuing such a strategy Carnival might risk straying from its core competence, there are two compelling reasons for considering diversification. First, there is an obvious similarity between cruise operations and resort operations. A second, more interesting, reason would be that in creating a Carnival-brand experience in another setting, Carnival could showcase its product and entice people to try a cruise. Just as Nike went into the business of hyperexperience retail stores called NikeTown to introduce people to the Nike brand in a dramatic way, Carnival could open a resort for low-penetration markets to introduce people to the brand and encourage them to try a cruise.

5. Carnival should concentrate on developing repeat customers by building a state-of-the-art customer relationship management system and providing incentives to its current customers to refer friends and family members. If it is

five times more costly to develop a new customer than it is to rebook a previous one, and every satisfied customer talks to at least four other people, the resulting drop in customer acquisition cost and increase in referral marketing would surely enhance brand profitability.

6. To remain the dominant player in the industry, Carnival must continue to expand on its tradition-breaking use of media. A Google keyword search for "Carnival Cruise Lines" resulted in two million hits, while one for "Royal Caribbean Cruise Lines" resulted in one million hits (even though the core brands are about the same size). If Carnival could manage the representation of its brand on these two million sites effectively, it would be positioned to exploit the full potential of the Internet to reach cruisers. Social media—exemplified by Facebook, Twitter, podcasting, and weblogs—offer massively popular, non-traditional "below-the-line" marketing communications channels that Carnival should explore.

7. Carnival's relationship with travel agents must be nurtured and protected. Because Carnival relies on travel agents for 80 percent of its business, it needs to concentrate on maintaining its good relationship with them. Possible opportunities include co-branding more visibly with one or more groups; offering more and better education and familiarization experiences; and becoming more sophisticated in tracking the effectiveness of the brand message, training, and promotions for travel agents who are representing the brand in the marketplace. An even more radical option might be to buy a chain of travel agencies.

8. Carnival brands some ships with the Carnival name but carries other names on others. Why the Holiday and Paradise lines are not branded as Carnival is not clear. Such brand inconsistency potentially confuses customers and compromises the umbrella endorsement of the Carnival brand. Either all these ships should be branded as Carnival or a separate brand needs to be created to encompass these non-Carnival ships with a clearly differentiated value proposition.

9. I am not sure that Walmart is the most appropriate brand metaphor for Carnival. The brand supremacy of the Walmart model has been supplanted by the more interesting and contemporary success of the Target model. While also capturing the value-conscious retail shopper, Target has done a much better job of creating excitement in the marketplace and has made a serious dent in both Walmart's and Kmart's market shares. Such value-oriented,

accessible-yet-stylish brand positioning would, I feel, better serve Carnival as a brand metaphor.

10. Carnival's market share should enable it to redefine its position in the cruise brandscape. There are several options for Carnival as it considers more interesting and "ownable" marketplace positions. One possibility would involve going head to head with Royal Caribbean's more active/thrill positioning. While the main advantage of such an option would be to steal market share by outspending Royal Caribbean, the main disadvantage would be that Royal Caribbean has been first to market and comes first to mind with this positioning. Yet there is a potential "flanking" opportunity that includes the active/theme position, which would be a natural evolution for Carnival. A more radical "flanking" position would be for Carnival to move to a passive/thrill position by offering entertainment options not available on most cruise ships.

In particular, Carnival needs to keep its eye on the possibility of targeting a younger demographic. A recent article in the *New York Times* reports, "While retirees are still a core segment of the cruise industry, the average age of passengers has fallen in the last decade to 50 from 60, according to the Cruise Line Industry Association in New York. The latest association survey shows that people under 40 now make up about a quarter of the manifest."[2] While the Carnival brand is well positioned to appeal to the younger cruiser, it is apparent that Royal Caribbean is actively promoting its brand to this demographic with its fast-paced onboard-adventure-themed "Get out there" advertising campaign.

11. Carnival should consider transitioning from being an international to being a truly *global* company. By expanding into markets such as the Pacific, Southeast Asia, and the Indian Ocean, it could offer its current customer more reasons to return and enable it to tap into the nascent but growing markets of India and China.

Summary

Carnival can retain its dominant status and strengthen its brand even though competition is fierce if it remains oriented toward the long term and does not flounder in the short term. In order to strengthen its brand, Carnival should continue its customer-centric focus by building better bonds with customers, providing a better value proposition than its competitors do, forging stronger relationships with travel agents, positioning itself against land-based options by stressing the cruise experience and considering operating its own land-based resorts, and expanding to new markets to give its past cruisers a reason to return and generate new customers.

---

1   This commentary draws upon and updates the author's prior research on and analysis of Carnival Cruise Lines. See Barbara-Jean Ross, Chekitan S. Dev, and Kathleen M. Dennison, "Carnival Cruise Lines: Teaching Note," in *Strategic Management Cases: Instructor's Manual,* ed. D. W. Grigsby and M. J. Stahl, 71–76 (Belmont, CA: Wadsworth, 1993).

2   Denny Lee, "Extreme Makeover: Taking High Style to the High Seas," *New York Times,* February 26, 2006, T8.

▶ PART TWO ◀

GLOBAL BRANDING

CHAPTER FOUR

Global Brand Expansion

When hotel firms expand internationally, they must choose ownership and management strategies that enable them to maintain their competitive advantages in a new market. The interplay between a company's strengths and local resources drives the type of partnership or affiliation arrangement that a company uses to enter a foreign market. This chapter follows recent research in assuming that the best entry strategy aligns an entering firm's strengths and weaknesses with a local market's environment as well as with the firm's own structural and strategic characteristics.[1]

The Challenge

When contemplating foreign market entry, any firm in any industry should separate ownership decisions from control decisions. The lodging industry has long separated ownership and management in its international locations. However, current industry structure means that decisions regarding ownership and management involve two steps.[2] First, an entering firm must decide whether to own the facilities in which its business will operate. Second, it must decide whether to manage a property itself, hire a management company, or seek local management.

Building on a prior study of international-market entry strategies, it is argued in this chapter that expanding hotel companies should also make separate ownership and control decisions for each business activity involved in the foreign operation.[3] Of special interest to the service industry are two particular business activities: investment in physical facilities and control of operations and marketing.

Perhaps the most important factor regarding international expansion in the hotel industry is an expanding firm's knowledge, which enables it to develop competitive advantages.[4] A firm's knowledge can be classified into two main types: *codified knowledge* and *tacit knowledge*. Codified knowledge—such as a firm's characteristic design features and signature service offerings—can be easily identified, structured, and communicated. Tacit knowledge—the firm's culture, workplace routines, and business processes—is less easily communicated.[5] This chapter investigates how a firm's competitive advantage, rooted in its codified and tacit knowledge, affects decisions regarding its foreign market entry strategy.

LOCAL PARTNERS IN FOREIGN MARKETS: TRANSFER AND ABSORPTION

In determining how to apply its knowledge-based competitive advantage to an international market, a hotel firm must understand how best to use that market's resources. More particularly, in seeking to transfer its codified and tacit knowledge to the foreign market, it needs to understand that market's capacity to absorb this know-how. If the local market cannot absorb transferred knowledge, a firm will not enjoy a competitive advantage in that market. Choosing how to enter a foreign market therefore depends on aligning the firm's advantages (and shortcomings) with the market's resources and business conditions. For each business activity the firm plans to conduct in the foreign market, it must decide on the best sorts of local partnerships to establish.

Determining how best to transfer codified and tacit knowledge rests therefore on developing a mutually beneficial partnership that combines a company's knowledge with knowledge held by local investors. Local partners of an entering firm can fill gaps in its understanding of the local market, and the local partners can tap into the firm's know-how to develop competitive advantages for themselves. The less able local partners are to provide knowledge or resources, the more the firm will need to exercise control over its operations in that market. By the same token, when an entering firm has little experience with or knowledge about a foreign market or potential partners there, the firms' resources and capabilities are at risk and the firm may fall victim to local opportunism. Under these conditions, such a firm will likely maintain control over its operations and ownership of its resources.

SEPARATING OWNERSHIP AND CONTROL

Historically, local expertise has been viewed in terms of production, distribution, and research and development (R&D). Because economic, technological, and competitive pressures have motivated firms to specialize in those activities for which they possess (or can readily acquire) a competitive advantage, many outsource the remainder of their business functions to partners who have complementary resources and know-how. In the hotel industry, such complementary assets and knowledge increasingly extend beyond production and distribution.

The decision process entails considering how several general business activities play out in terms of vulnerability to opportunism and the transferability of know-how. Some may entail relatively high risks of local-partner opportunism (R&D, plant and equipment, marketing); others are relatively easy to transfer to local partners (plant and equipment, distribution). A firm must balance vulnerability and ease of transfer in determining whether to own or invest in local facilities or resources and how much control to exercise over marketing and operations. Within a particular general function, say, marketing, an entering firm should undertake high-risk activities itself (in the case of branding, for instance, which is difficult to transfer) while outsourcing low-risk, easy-to-transfer activities, such as pricing, to local partners.[6]

FOUR VARIATIONS ON OWNERSHIP AND CONTROL

Given that ownership and control are separable, there are four models or types of arrangements between entering firms and local partners to consider. For example, local investors who lack industry expertise can purchase land and build facilities for a hotel firm to manage. Alternatively, a hotel firm can finance the purchase and construction of its own facilities. Such a firm may then approach marketing and operations by applying its own policies and procedures to the local infrastructure. In yet another approach, a hotel firm relies on the expertise of a franchise system or marketing network to guide its local marketing and operations. If we combine these two dimensions regarding international hotel expansion, we can distinguish foreign market entrants with an ownership stake in a local hotel from those that have no such stake. Local hotels can be categorized according to whether marketing and operations follow the policies and procedures of a franchise system or third-party marketing network or whether the firms apply their own policies and procedures. If we then combine these decisions relating to ownership with decisions relating to marketing and operations, we see that a company has four possible market entry strategies.

Chain-owned, affiliated (COA) hotels are operated as part of a franchise system or marketing network. Here the market entrant invests in the physical assets of these hotels while relying (at least in part) on the franchise system or marketing network to guide its marketing and operations activities. *Management company, affiliated* (MCA) hotels are operated by a third-party management company and also linked with a franchise system or marketing network; in this situation the entering firm does not hold an equity position in the hotel facility. Here again, MCA hotels are subject to the marketing and operations policies of the system or network. *Management company, unaffiliated* (MCU) hotels are operated under management contracts but have no affiliation with franchise systems or marketing networks. Hotels in this category develop an in-house approach to marketing and operations. *Chain-owned, unaffiliated* (COU) hotels are owned and operated under a common brand name as part of a corporate chain. They are independent of both third-party management companies and franchise systems. The COU entry strategy therefore offers a firm the highest level of control of the hotel's marketing and operations functions.

The Study

This study tested hypotheses corresponding to the four abovementioned categories of foreign market entry while controlling for other factors such as a local market's potential for growth, its general business conditions, the sociocultural distance separating the home market from the foreign market, and the size of the entering firm. The sample consisted of 124 hotel managers who had worked on at least three continents representing more than thirty internationally oriented hotel brands distributed across fifty-three countries.

To determine respondents' foreign market entry strategies, two questions were posed. First, respondents were asked to specify their property's type of firm. Second, respondents were asked whether the property belonged to a franchise system or a marketing network. Only parent companies that operated more than one hotel at the time of the study were included. The responses were sorted according to the four entry strategies identified above (COA, MCA, MCU, and COU). All measurements of these and other variables met the usual statistical standards of reliability and validity.

Results

The study applied a resource-based perspective to the market entry decision, thereby focusing on three factors: (a) an entering firm's ability to transfer its know-how (codified and tacit) to the local market, (b) potential local partners' ability to absorb that know-how, and (c) the availability of qualified and trustworthy investment partners in the local market. In determining its entry strategy in a foreign market, a firm will choose the strategy that best allows it to transfer its competitive advantages to that market. In the hotel industry, such competitive advantages are based largely on a firm's knowledge, whether codified or tacit.

In our research we investigated the following types of hotel knowledge: (a) the ability to generate customer service, (b) superior company management and organization, and (c) distinctive and effective physical facilities. The first two reflect a market entrant's tacit knowledge while the third exemplifies its codified knowledge.

Customer Service

To generate effective customer service, a firm seeks to create and maintain an adequate customer base while ensuring customer satisfaction. Transferring the advantages of excellent customer service into a foreign market requires considerable managerial, human, and financial resources. This in turn requires a firm to exercise a high degree of control over its operations to prevent a local partner from shirking its responsibilities or cutting corners. As a consequence, firms with a competitive advantage based on customer service will maintain control over their foreign operations, in particular their marketing activities and operations. However, because such a competitive advantage is largely unrelated to ownership, a firm with a strong competitive advantage in customer service is unlikely to affiliate with an outside brand or chain (COU >COA; MCU >MCA).

The results regarding this measure indicate that an entrant's customer service advantage is more likely to be associated with the MCU entry strategy than with any of the others—COU, COA, or MCA. The latter case, MCU >MCA, supports the expectation that a firm needs to exercise considerable managerial control over marketing and operations to protect its customer service competitive advantage.

Company Management and Organization

Superior managerial and organizational expertise can provide a competitive advantage. Such an advantage aids a firm in satisfying the predilections of its target market as well as in achieving cost leadership. Here again, such expertise is largely a function of tacit knowledge and is therefore difficult to transfer into a foreign market. The transfer of such managerial assets as effective decision heuristics, written rules and procedures, and a management information system cannot be accomplished without a firm's controlling its marketing and operations. This is impractical in the context of a franchising or marketing-network arrangement. As was the case with customer service, a firm that enjoys a competitive advantage in management and organization is likely to choose an entry strategy characterized by a high level of control over marketing and operations (COU >COA; MCU >MCA).

The results regarding this measure indicate that the stronger the competitive advantage a firm enjoys in management and organization the less likely it is to apply the COA entry strategy as compared with the COU strategy (COU >COA), the MCA strategy (MCA >COA), or the MCU strategy (MCU >COA). Only the first case is consistent with expectations. The three results taken together suggest that an affiliation with a franchise system or marketing network constrains a chain's ability to transfer its competitive advantage in management and organization to its owned hotels.

Physical Facilities

In the hotel industry, physical facilities that embody the decor and design of a property are tangible symbols of the intangible elements of the lodging experience that a firm offers to its customers. This means that the knowledge involved in a firm's characteristic, brand-specific physical design elements are easy to codify and therefore easy to transfer to a foreign market. On the face of it, then, a firm with such a competitive advantage should seek to avoid the commitment of financial and managerial resources that are involved in owner-ship. Yet there is no guarantee that local owners will build physical facilities to match the specifications set by an entering firm. Local owners may stray from signature design elements, reducing or eliminating the firm's competitive advantage. Therefore, under such conditions, an entering firm will likely maintain some form or degree of ownership of physical facilities (COA >MCA; COU >MCU). Since its expertise in physical facilities design and execution is independent of its marketing and operations functions, even when it owns the property a firm might accept a relatively low level of control over these functions (MCA >MCU; COA >COU).[7]

The study results indicate that firms with an advantage in physical facilities are more likely to choose the COA entry strategy as compared with the others (COA >COU, COA >MCA, COA >MCU). These results also suggest that entrants with such a competitive advantage are indeed likely to select an entry strategy featuring lower control over marketing and operations.

When choosing a foreign market entry strategy, a firm must consider not only the transferability of its own knowledge but also the absorptive capacity of the local market's potential business partners. Transfer depends on the availability of local human resources, the cost of training, and the availability of reliable local suppliers.

Availability of Resources. Clearly, in markets with plentiful local resources, entering firms can easily transfer their own knowledge, avoid opportunistic local partners, and therefore apply strategies that involve relatively lower degrees of marketing and operational control (MCA >MCU; COA >COU). Again, the results partially support this expectation. Firms in this situation are more likely to use the COA strategy than the COU strategy (COA >COU) and are more likely to choose the MCU strategy than they are the MCA strategy (MCU >MCA). However, of those two preferred strategies, entrants unexpectedly are more likely to select the COA strategy than they are the MCU strategy (COA >MCU).

Cost of Local-Partner Training. Obviously, high training costs make knowledge transfer expensive and thereby reduce the associated competitive advantage. Since such higher training costs are likely due to a scarcity of qualified local employees, an entering firm facing high training costs should be inclined to choose an entry strategy that features relatively high levels of control over marketing and operations (COU >COA; MCU >MCA). Note that, here again, there are no ownership implications related to training costs.[8]

The results again provide partial support for this prediction. Entrants facing high training costs are more likely to use the MCU strategy than they are the MCA strategy (MCU >MCA), as expected. They are also more likely to use the MCU strategy than they are the COU strategy (MCU >COU), which is contrary to expectations but consistent with the spirit of the prediction.

Availability of Trustworthy, Reliable Local Investment Partners. An entering firm has little choice but to make an equity investment if a local market lacks trustworthy, reliable investment partners. Unqualified investment partners expose the entrant to an increased risk of opportunism and incompetence. Consequently, when a local market offers a pool of qualified investment partners, an entering firm can choose an entry strategy that requires a lower level of equity participation (MCA >COA; MCU >COU). Since this choice carries no control implications beyond the issue of investment equity, it has no bearing on the degree of control needed vis-à-vis marketing and operations.[9]

The only telling result here is that the more qualified are the available investors in a local market the more likely it is that a firm will choose the COA entry strategy over the MCA strategy (COA >MCA), as expected.

Actionable Insights

When it comes to marketing-entry strategies surrounding the separation of ownership from managerial control, the study demonstrates the benefits of separating those decisions. For example, the usual prescription is to retain ownership in foreign markets where the cost of training local employees is high. A hotel facing such a situation should retain control over a local facility's marketing and operations but avoid owning the facility. This spares the entrant the heavy investment required of ownership yet still provides the firmer control needed to cope with high training costs. A similar prescription applies to firms that have a competitive advantage based on superior customer service—control can be gained without ownership.

Interestingly, a hotel firm's competitive advantage based on its management and organization can be transferred to local markets using several entry modes—in particular, the COU, MCU, and MCA entry modes. Only the COA entry mode is not useful in transferring a management-and-organization competitive advantage to local markets. This suggests that the dictates of a franchising system or marketing network hinder an entrant's ability to transfer its tacit competitive advantages, specifically its management-and-organizational advantage.

The study strongly suggests that the ownership dimension of an entry decision is associated with a local market's capacity to absorb an entering firm's competitive advantages. For example, when trustworthy and reliable local equity partners are available (the absorptive capacity of the local equity market is high), a firm should use a management company entry strategy rather than equity ownership to transfer its competitive advantages. Such a strategy is also recommended when the cost of training managers and employees in a local market is high (the market's absorptive capacity is low). In this situation, an entering firm can capitalize on a management company's expertise in hiring and managing human resources, thereby avoiding the high costs of hiring and training local employees.

When a local market's absorptive capacity for operations is high, an entering firm can transfer its tacit competitive advantages through some form of marketing affiliation because local resources are readily available. Lower-control entry strategies are the choice when local human resources are abundant.

Finally, in seeking to transfer a competitive advantage based on codifiable knowledge embodied in physical facilities, chain ownership of a hotel property is the best choice, especially when the entering firm is affiliated with a franchise system or marketing network. This finding suggests that an entering firm can build hotels to its specifications more easily by retaining ownership rather than by opting for the management company entry strategy.

---

1 See Iketchi Ekeledo and K. Sivakumar, "Foreign Market Entry Mode Choice of Service Firms: A Contingency Perspective," *Journal of the Academy of Marketing Science* 26, no. 4 (1998): 274–92; Peter Hwang and W. Chan Kim, "An Eclectic Theory of the Choice of International Entry Mode," *Strategic Management Journal* 11, no. 2 (1990): 117–28.

2 Yigang Pan and David K. Tse, "The Hierarchical Model of Market Entry Modes," *Journal of International Business Studies* 31, no. 4 (2000): 535–54.

3 The prior study is Chekitan S. Dev, M. Krishna Erramilli, and Sanjeev Agarwal, "Brands across Borders: Choosing between Franchising and Management Contracts for Entering International Markets," *Cornell Hotel and Restaurant Administration Quarterly* 43, no. 6 (2002): 91–104.

4 Many factors tied into competitive advantage that affect foreign entry decisions have been identified recently; among these factors are (a) market concentration or diversification strategy; (b) global concentration, synergy, and strategic motivations; (c) other strategic factors, such as the importance of scale economies, quality control, reservations systems, and training investment; and (d) imperfectly imitable capabilities vis-à-vis nonequity entry strategies (e.g., franchising versus management services contracts).

5 Bruce Kogut and Ugo Zander, "Knowledge of the Firm, Combinative Capabilities, and the Replication of Technology," *Organization Science* 3, no. 3 (1992): 383–97; Anoop Madhok, "Cost, Value, and Foreign Market Entry Mode: The Transaction and the Firm," *Strategic Management Journal* 18, no. 1 (1997): 39–61.

6 M. Krishna Erramilli, Sanjeev Agarwal, and Chekitan S. Dev, "Choice between Non-equity Entry Modes: An Organizational Capability Perspective," *Journal of International Business Studies* 33, no. 2 (2002): 223–42.

7 See Kathleen R. Conner and C. K. Prahalad, "A Resource-Based Theory of the Firm: Knowledge versus Opportunism," *Organization Science* 7, no. 5 (1996): 477–501.

8 See Daniel C. Bello and David I. Gilliland, "The Effect of Output Controls, Process Controls, and Flexibility on Export Channel Performance," *Journal of Marketing* 61, no. 1 (1997): 22–38; and Farok J. Contractor and Sumit K. Kundu, "Modal Choice in a World of Alliances: Analyzing Organizational Forms in the International Hotel Sector," *Journal of International Business Studies* 29, no. 2 (1998): 325–58.

9 See Erin Anderson and Hubert Gatignon, "Modes of Foreign Entry: A Transaction Cost Analysis and Propositions," *Journal of International Business Studies* 17, no. 3 (1986): 1–26; Yadong Luo, *Entry and Cooperative Strategies in International Business Expansion* (Westport, CT: Quorum Books, 1999).

CHAPTER FIVE

Branding beyond Borders

 otel brands commonly enter international markets through contractual arrangements such as franchises and management contracts.[1] The study presented in this chapter examines the factors that brands consider in choosing between franchising or management contracts. The study considers firm assets such as machinery, process know-how, and trade resources and skills as well as environmental factors that influence this choice.[2]

The Challenge

The choice between using franchising or management contracts for hotel brand expansion is difficult to explain using traditional international-business theories, because hotel brands care more about the effective transfer of technology and deployment of transaction-specific assets or knowledge than about the possible dissipation of such assets or knowledge. Such transfer is essential to maintaining consistency of brand image and operations. Therefore, hotel brands care less about control and more about the effectiveness of transfer. To address this issue, this chapter's study adopts a novel framework based on an organizational-capabilities perspective, an approach that focuses on the transfer of one firm's competencies to another.

ORGANIZATIONAL CAPABILITIES

The organizational-capabilities perspective has emerged from a growing emphasis in strategic-management research on the resource-based view of a firm's performance. This resource-based view exemplifies a shift in research emphasis toward features that create competitive advantages for individual firms. On this view, a firm's superior performance is a consequence of its distinctive capabilities rather than of the structural properties of its industry.

Resources and Capabilities

The capabilities-based approach regards every firm as a bundle of resources that comprise all of the firm's assets, organizational processes, attributes, information, and expertise.[3] Firm resources can be generally classified into three categories: (a) physical (plant, equipment, location, brands, patents, and trademarks), (b) human (the skills and knowledge of individual employees), and (c) organizational (culture, routines, and rituals).[4]

A hotel brand can be regarded as having twenty-two resources that might drive its competitive advantage.[5] These resources can be combined into higher-order capabilities: (a) organizational competence, (b) quality competence, (c) customer competence, (d) entry competence, and (e) physical competence. *Organizational* competence captures skills and capabilities that enable a brand to compete effectively (corporate culture, empowerment, operating policies and procedures, reservation systems). *Quality* competence includes skills and capabilities needed to offer high-quality service and ensure customer satisfaction. *Customer* competence encompasses capabilities that help a hotel brand create its reputation, establish a customer base, and build customer loyalty. *Entry* competence taps a brand's ability to find good locations and to time its market entry advantageously. Finally, *physical* competence captures a brand's ability to design and build physical facilities with desirable quality, comfort, and ambience.

Effects of Capabilities on Choice

Understanding how the capabilities-based approach might help a hotel brand's managers choose between a franchise arrangement and a management contract begins with analyzing the factors that distinguish franchising from management contracting. Chief among these is the extent of technology transfer. Under a franchise arrangement an entering brand relies heavily on the franchisee's capabilities; under a management contract the entering brand provides most of the day-to-day managerial and technical support. Under franchising, then, a brand transfers resources and expertise across firm boundaries, whereas under management contracts it transfers such assets within the firm. If we can understand the factors that influence the effective transfer of a brand's resources, we can better understand how brands might choose between franchising and management contracts.

Factors Affecting the Transfer of
Resources and Capabilities

The capabilities-based perspective measures the value of a resource or capability in terms of its contribution to a firm's competitive advantage.[6] Obviously, when a hotel brand enters another country, it must transfer its resources and capabilities to its foreign operations. At the same time, however, the brand wants to ensure that the transfer of such assets does not diminish its ability to generate the desired competitive advantage. The question is, What difference would it make to choose a franchising arrangement rather than a management contract?

According to the capabilities-based approach, resources or capabilities need not be transferred within a firm unless a resource or capability is in some way unique to, or ideally suited to, that particular firm's practices and is therefore difficult to imitate or reproduce.[7] By definition, then, an irreproducible resource or capability is difficult or impossible for the host country collaborator to absorb or replicate without losing or reducing the associated competitive advantage. In such cases a brand is highly likely to transfer the resource or capability internally.

Some capabilities are more difficult to reproduce than others. Among the factors often cited as preventing one brand from replicating another brand's resources and capabilities are specific historical conditions, complex social interactions, and the tacit (intangible) nature of the know-how involved.[8] It is widely acknowledged that transferring tacit knowledge is difficult: it is complex; it is acquired through trial and error; it is taught and learned by demonstration, observation, imitation, practice, and feedback; and it is continuously evolving.

Some resources and capabilities are said to be embedded in a firm. An embedded capability is deeply entrenched in company-specific routines and practices, shaping complex social interactions and team relationships. The knowledge embodied in such a capability can be transferred only through intimate social interactions. Furthermore, the transfer of such embedded knowledge requires transferring the established routines and organizational processes through which the knowledge is applied.[9]

Franchising or Management Contracts?

A firm typically possesses a mix of reproducible competencies (entry, physical, and customer) and irreproducible competencies (quality and organizational).

A hotel brand that expands by transferring irreproducible competencies that provide it with a competitive advantage should favor management contracts because any attempted transfer of such competencies within the context of a franchising arrangement could reduce or eliminate that competitive advantage. Moreover, the influence of such irreproducible competencies on the choice between franchising and management contracts depends on the strength of the associated competitive advantage. When such competencies do not generate value for a brand and are difficult to transfer to a host market, however, they are not likely to influence the brand's choice. On the other hand, when such capabilities are critical to the brand's competitive advantage, they will dominate the decision-making process. It seems likely therefore that the greater is the competitive advantage generated by a brand's irreproducible competencies, the more likely it is that the brand will choose a management contract over franchising.[10]

OTHER FACTORS

Several other factors enter into the decision of whether to enter a market via franchising or management contracts, including the availability of management capabilities in the host market, the availability of suitable partners, and the development level of the host country's business environment.

Management Availability. In addition to accounting for a host hotel's capacity to reproduce a brand's resources and capabilities, the capabilities-based perspective stresses the role of the supporting local infrastructure in facilitating or impeding the transfer of the entering firm's resources and capabilities.[11] For example, franchising is not conducive to exploiting an entering brand's advantages if a host country's franchisees lack ready access to competent managers. Thus, a brand should be more likely to choose a management contract over a franchising arrangement when qualified managerial employees are not readily available in the host market.

Availability of Partners. Management contracts succeed only if a hotel management firm can find qualified and trustworthy partners with complementary capabilities—that is, collaborators who can make the necessary capital investments in infrastructure and facilities and thereby free up the foreign firm to focus on managing the brand. Without qualified and trustworthy investment partners, it is much more difficult to establish effective management contracts.[12] Thus, the ready availability of trustworthy and qualified investment partners in a host market should increase the likelihood that an entering brand will choose a management contract over a franchising arrangement.

Business Environment. Effective transfer of resources and capabilities depends not only on the characteristics of an entering brand, but also—sometimes crucially—on the capabilities of the host country collaborator. Those capabilities, in turn, depend on the general business environment within which the host organization will be operating. Consequently, franchising is more effective and franchisees are more capable in developed countries than in developing ones.[13] If a high level of development in the local business environment encourages franchising generally, then it stands to reason that franchising becomes more viable in relation to management contracts when the host market's business environment is highly developed.

SUMMARY OF FACTORS

This analysis based on the organizational-capability approach has identified four factors that should influence a hotel firm's choice between franchising and management contracts when entering foreign markets, yielding the following guidelines: (1) the presence of irreproducible resources and capabilities favors management contracts over franchising; (2) the availability of management resources in a host market favors franchising arrangements over management contracts; (3) the availability of qualified local investment partners in a host market favors management contracts over franchising; and (4) a highly developed business environment favors franchising arrangements over management contracts.

The Study

SURVEY QUESTIONNAIRE

The study is based on a survey of hotel managers in foreign markets. Following an initial mailing of 530 questionnaires to such managers, the final sample consisted of 139 respondents working at hotel brands operated under either pure franchising arrangements or pure management contracts. More than thirty brands distributed over forty-six countries are represented in the study.

In addition to testing for the four factors listed above under the heading "Summary of Factors," the study also tested for several control factors: (1) the size of the hotel brand serving the foreign market, (2) the hotel brand's international experience, (3) the size of the subsidiary hotel property, (4) the reputation of the hotel brand in the host market, and (5) the level of service sensitivity of the hotel brand's target audience.

MEASURING CAPABILITIES

For a determination of whether the five capabilities identified earlier in the chapter are distinct, respondents rated the extent to which their brands enjoyed a competitive advantage in each of the twenty-two resources on a scale anchored by 1 (no advantage) and 5 (great advantage), which confirmed the existence of the five overarching competencies (organizational, quality, customer, entry, and physical).

To determine which of these competencies is irreproducible, firms in foreign markets that were collaborating with entry firms were asked to rate the extent to which they believed they could imitate the entry firm's overall competitive advantage. A statistical analysis of the responses indicated that organizational competence and quality competence are the largest contributors to the irreproducibility of a firm's competitive advantage, while customer, entry, and physical competencies do not play the same role in the irreproducibility of a firm's competitive advantage.

TESTING THE MAIN EFFECTS
OF COMPETENCIES ON CHOICE

Statistical analysis of questionnaire responses was used to test whether the five competencies influenced the choice between franchising and management contracts as predicted by the organizational-capabilities perspective. The tests included three external control variables: (1) the availability of management capabilities in a host market, (2) the availability of investment partners in a host market, and (3) the development level of the host country's business environment. There were five internal control variables: (1) the size of the foreign entrant, (2) international experience of the foreign entrant, (3) host property size, (4) host property's reputation, and (5) service sensitivity of the target audience.

TESTING CONTINGENT OR COMBINED EFFECTS

The competencies included in the study could have complex interactive effects with internal or external control variables in determining the advantage-generating choice between franchising and management contracts. In other words, it is important to understand how competencies affect the choice of business model in conjunction with other factors. The study therefore tested the following joint effects: (1) interaction of organizational competence and the level of development in a host market, (2) entrant brand's reputation and physical competence, (3) quality competence and the service sensitivity of the market, (4) quality competence and the size of the local hotel property.

Results

COMPETENCIES AS INDEPENDENT FACTORS

The results of the main-effects tests suggest that irreproducible capabilities—organizational competence and quality competence—influence the choice between franchising and management contracting in the direction of management contracts as the contribution these two capabilities make to a brand's competitive advantage increases. Again, as expected, the other capabilities—customer competence, entry competence, and physical competence—showed no significant effect on the franchising–management contract choice. Taken together, these results strongly support the contention that irreproducibility is a key factor in choosing management contracts over franchising.

The results also indicate that choosing a management contract over a franchising arrangement becomes more likely as managerial talent becomes scarcer and investment collaborators become more abundant in the host country. In addition, the results suggest that franchising is preferred as the host country business environment becomes increasingly developed.

It is interesting to note that there was no direct effect arising from any of the internal control factors. This shows that the choice between a management contract and franchising does not depend on the size of a hotel firm, its international experience, the size or reputation of the local property, or the service sensitivity of the target market.

COMBINED EFFECTS OF COMPETENCIES

First, although brand entrants seem to prefer franchising when the host business environment is highly developed, the preference switches to management contracts when organizational competence makes an increasingly greater contribution to their competitive advantage. The probability of choosing management contracts is extremely high in poorly developed markets and drops dramatically in favor of franchising in highly developed markets—but only when organizational competence is not important to competitive advantage. When organizational competence is important, management contracts continue to be strongly favored regardless of market conditions.

Second, while physical competence alone may not influence the selection of franchising, it can become a powerful predictor in conjunction with strong brand reputation. When physical competence provides a competitive advantage, franchising is strongly favored only when the brand's reputation is also strong in the host market. If the brand is weak, by contrast, the probability of using a management contract increases.

Third, a brand's preference for a management contract strengthens with the rising importance of quality competence in large hotels. Generally speaking, when quality competence provides a competitive advantage, the tendency to choose a management contract strengthens as the hotel increases in size. However, when quality provides no competitive advantage, management contracts are less preferred and franchising becomes more likely as hotel size increases.

Finally, the influence of quality competence on the choice of a management contract or franchising becomes stronger when the hotel's market tends to be service sensitive. In markets where customers have low service expectations, the company's quality competence makes no difference. However, when customer service expectations are high, brands are more likely to choose management contracts if they possess a competitive advantage in quality competence, but tilt towards franchising if they don't.

The results of the study also show that, among other things, customer competence—which played a minor role in the results of the main-effects tests—figures prominently in the model that includes interactions among variables. Evidently, the preference for management contracts is stronger when the advantage generated by strong customer competence is higher.

Actionable Insights

How can brand managers facing the choice between franchising and management contracts in the course of international expansion use these results? Brands that follow the lead of the successful multinational hotel brands that were surveyed should do well initiating international expansion. Prior to the study reported in this chapter, relatively little was known about the criteria that hotel brands apply in choosing between franchising and management contracts. This study addressed that gap in the literature using the organizational-capability perspective to explain a hotel brand's choice between a franchise arrangement and a management contract.

The results strongly support the capabilities-based view that irreproducible capabilities such as organizational competence and quality competence cannot be transferred effectively through franchising. The difficulty of reproducing competencies not only protects a brand from its competitors, it also thwarts its efforts to transfer the needed capabilities to associates and collaborators in the host market, "forcing" it to employ such mechanisms as management contracts.[14]

The main lesson to be learned from our results is that as hotel brands expand internationally, they must focus on two main points in choosing between franchising and management contracts. First, such a brand should ascertain the distribution of its key competencies across the five areas identified in this study. Second, the brand should ascertain the extent to which it depends on irreproducible competencies for its competitive advantage.

If irreproducible competencies support a brand's establishment and survival, that brand should expand using management contracts. On the other hand, franchising requires relatively little involvement by the entering company. Therefore, franchising suffices as long as the key aspects of a hotel brand can be codified and transferred. For example, it is relatively easy to transfer the physical ambience required for establishing a certain stated quality of construction and for projecting a consistent brand image. Moreover, the strategy of selecting appropriate locations that preempt others can still be implemented. Thus, as long as there is no specific knowledge or skill that comes in the form of managerial expertise, requisite knowledge can be transferred through a franchise arrangement. Note that the transfer of easy-to-reproduce capabilities does not appear to play a strong direct role here, since those capabilities can be transferred equally effectively via both management contracts and franchise arrangements. This finding suggests, perhaps, that the difference in transfer costs between franchising and management contracts is not large enough to produce unambiguous choices.

The results also corroborate the contention that brands need a range of internal and external support capabilities to exploit their advantages.[15] For instance, franchising is favored in developed countries and in those with an abundance of professional managers. When professional managers are scarce, brands must make up for the shortfall through internal transfers rather than by selling franchises. Resource effectiveness is as critical as availability. The easier it is to find franchisees with high levels of competence and "absorptive capacity," the more advisable it is for entering brands to choose franchising. Franchising is also favored when a brand has both high physical competence and a strong brand reputation. Physical competence and a strong brand reputation work together in a way that unambiguously favors franchising.[16]

It is when reliable investment partners are easy to find in a host market that management contracts become increasingly attractive, especially for large firms or large hotel properties. In addition, scale effects emerge when quality competence and hotel size are combined. Our results suggest that as quality competence becomes more important as a source of competitive advantage, a brand's desire for a management contract varies with the size of the hotel property. Evidently, the know-how needed to offer quality service becomes increasingly complex as the hotel property expands in size, thus making a management contract all the more necessary to transfer key capabilities to the host market.[17]

Management contracts are also favored when an entering firm combines high-quality competence with a service-sensitive market. The interaction between quality competence and service sensitivity highlights the interplay between internal capabilities and external market requirements, a noted strength of resource- and capability-based approaches.[18] As a hotel's customers become increasingly service conscious and demand better and better amenities, hotels with a strong quality competence become increasingly committed to management contracts.

Finally, management contracts are favored when a brand has strong organizational competence and enters a highly developed market. The results suggest that brands are driven primarily by the transferability of their advantageous capabilities when choices are made between franchising and management contracts. When these capabilities are irreproducible, firms not only shun franchise arrangements but also become strong advocates for management contracts in developed markets. In other words, while external support capabilities are important, the choice appears to be driven primarily by internal capability considerations.

---

1 John H. Dunning, *Explaining International Production* (London: Unwin Hyman, 1988), 242–65.

2 Farok J. Contractor and Sumit K. Kundu, "Modal Choice in a World of Alliances: Analyzing Organizational Forms in the International Hotel Sector," *Journal of International Business Studies* 29, no. 2 (1998): 325–58.

3 Jay Barney, "Firm Resources and Sustained Competitive Advantage," *Journal of Management* 17, no. 1 (1991): 99–120.

4 Ibid.

5 This is based on addition to our industry knowledge and communications with hotel managers as well as Gaylen N. Chandler and Steven H. Hanks, "Market Attractiveness, Resource-Based Capabilities, Venture Strategies, and Venture Performance," *Journal of Business Venturing* 9, no. 4 (1994): 331–49.

6 David J. Collis and Cynthia A. Montgomery, "Competing on Resources: Strategy in the 1990s," *Harvard Business Review* 73, no. 4 (1995): 118–28; and Anoop Madhok, "Cost, Value, and Foreign Market Entry Mode: The Transaction and the Firm," *Strategic Management Journal* 18, no. 1 (1997): 39–61.

7 Madhok uses the term "imperfect imitability" in "Cost, Value, and Foreign Market Entry Mode," 45, 46, 47.

8 Barney, "Firm Resources and Sustained Competitive Advantage"; Yao-Su Hu, "The International Transferability of the Firm's Advantages," *California Management Review* 37, no. 4 (1995): 73–88; Bruce Kogut and Udo Zander, "Knowledge of the Firm and the Evolutionary Theory of the Multinational Corporation," *Journal of International Business Studies* 24, no. 4 (1993): 625–46; and David J. Teece, "Capturing Value from Knowledge Assets: The New Economy, Markets for Know-How, and Intangible Assets," *California Management Review* 40, no. 3 (1998): 55–79.

9 Alice Lam, "Embedded Firms, Embedded Knowledge: Problems of Collaboration and Knowledge Transfer in Global Cooperative Ventures," *Organization Studies* 18, no. 6 (1997): 973–96; and Madhok, "Cost, Value, and Foreign Market Entry Mode."

10 A brand can sustain its competitive advantage even with no irreproducible competencies, through, for example, legal means such as copyrights, trademarks, patents, and licenses, but this chapter concentrates on the relationship between the reproducibility of competencies and the franchising/management contract choice.

11 Hu, "The International Transferability of the Firm's Advantages"; and Madhok, "Cost, Value, and Foreign Market Entry Mode."

12 Contractor and Kundu, "Modal Choice in a World of Alliances"; and Dunning, *Explaining International Production.*

13 Farok J. Contractor and Sumit K. Kundu, "Franchising versus Company-Run Operations: Modal Choice in the Global Hotel Sector," *Journal of International Marketing* 6, no. 2 (1998): 28–53.

14 Ashish Arora and Andrea Fosfuri, "Wholly Owned Subsidiary versus Technology Licensing in the Worldwide Chemical Industry," *Journal of International Business Studies* 3, no. 4 (2000): 555–72; and Kogut and Zander, "Knowledge of the Firm."

15 Hu, "The International Transferability of the Firm's Advantages"; and Madhok, "Cost, Value, and Foreign Market Entry Mode."

16 Arora and Fosfuri, "Wholly Owned Subsidiary versus Technology Licensing"; and Kogut and Zander, "Knowledge of the Firm."

17 Hubert Gatignon and Erin Anderson, "The Multinational Corporations' Degree of Control over Foreign Subsidiaries: An Empirical Test of a Transaction Cost Explanation," *Journal of Law, Economics, and Organization* 4, no. 2 (1988) 305–36; Scott A. Shane, "Hybrid Organizational Arrangements and Their Implications for Firm Growth and Survival: A Study of New Franchisors," *Academy of Management Journal* 39, no. 1 (1996): 216–34.

18 Collis and Montgomery, "Competing on Resources."

CHAPTER SIX

Brand Strategies

B y adopting a market orientation, a brand commits itself to satisfying its customers' needs over the long run. Although profitability, market share, return on investment, and other performance benchmarks ultimately determine the success of any strategy, a market orientation is meant to achieve such goals by providing customers with superior value on a sustained basis. Those familiar with the concept understand that adopting a market orientation is not merely undertaking a marketing department initiative, but instead means instituting an organization-wide culture that, when properly established, provides a brand with norms and beliefs that shape an integrated organizational strategy for sensing changing customer demand and competitive challenges, as well as anticipating future market conditions.

The Challenge

Business scholars established the theoretical usefulness of the market orientation concept in seminal articles published over twenty years ago, but much work remains in refining the concept so as to render empirical results achieved with its application that are useful to corporate executive and management teams.[1] This chapter presents a study that offered an opportunity not only to contribute some important results to the theoretical literature but also to provide some practical information to global hotel managers looking to implement the most advantageous strategy in overseas markets.

In two groundbreaking papers, Ajay Kohli and Bernard Jaworski, and John Narver and Stanley Slater laid down the canonical view of the market orientation. On their view such an orientation combines three main components: a *customer orientation,* through which a brand strives to understand its target customers; a *competitor orientation,* through which a brand strives to understand what its competitors are doing; and *interfunctional coordination,* the organizational culture that orients employees in all departments of a business unit to understanding the brand's market in terms of both customers and competitors.[2] There is widespread consensus that such a strategic orientation can create "superior value" for customers and thereby generate "continuous superior performance" for a brand.[3]

Although most people accept that a market orientation is efficacious, several theoretical issues remain alive. This chapter addresses three of these issues—the extent to which the efficacy of a market orientation depends on environmental factors; whether, within a market orientation, a brand should concentrate more of its resources on being customer oriented or on being competitor oriented; and how being in a global market plays into the effectiveness of a market orientation. To test the effects of environmental factors on a market orientation, the hypotheses developed for the study assume what is known as the *contingency approach;* that is, the study was designed to test whether the results of a market orientation depend on environmental conditions. The study also compares the effects of being customer oriented with those of being competitor oriented under a range of market conditions. The chapter concludes with several important implications that bear directly on marketing strategy in the global hotel market.

Testing the contingency aspect, that is, the degree to which a market orientation is affected by environmental factors, was guided by a recent study on the effectiveness of both a customer orientation and a competitor orientation for various market conditions at different levels of economic activity.[4] Thus, the hypotheses were tested at the country level to reflect stages of economic development, at the local market level to reflect local business conditions and resource availability, and at the consumer level to reflect vagaries of customer demand. This enabled the study to address all three targeted research areas: the effectiveness of a market orientation in various market conditions, the comparative effectiveness of a customer and a competitor orientation within a market orientation, and the effectiveness of a market orientation in a global marketplace (that of the hotel industry with its diversity of economic, cultural, and other environmental conditions). The effectiveness of interfunctional coordination was tested only as a control variable. The greatest focus was on customer versus competitor orientation.

Hypothesizing Customer versus Competitor Orientation

Four sets of hypotheses were developed to test the contingency view of market orientation. If this view is correct, no single corporate strategy for achieving a brand's benchmark performance goals or competitive advantage is universally effective under all market conditions. Instead, a brand should gain competitive advantage by matching its strategy to both external and internal environmental conditions. This study concentrated on external conditions (as reflected in treating interfunctional coordination as a control variable). George Day and Robin Wensley, for example, argue that when market demand is predictable and the competitive environment is stable and concentrated, brands should channel more of their resources toward a competitor orientation. In contrast, in a dynamic market with many competitors, highly segmented customers, and shifting entry barriers, brands should orient their strategy more in the direction of understanding their customer base.[5]

A customer orientation can facilitate differentiation in a market. The strategy is to gather information from and about a brand's customers, information that is then disseminated throughout the brand's organization to enable it to appeal to as many customer segments in its market as possible. A competitor orientation can achieve cost advantages for a brand, as it gathers information on its competitors' business practices, enabling it to reduce costs through adjustments to its value chain. The contingency view is that environmental conditions that characterize a brand's market—especially pertaining to its customer base and competitive set—inevitably determine whether customer intelligence or competitor intelligence has a greater influence on the brand's ability to achieve a competitive advantage. The hypotheses in this study therefore reflect two sets of environmental differences by considering the market's stage of economic development, resource availability, and how demanding customers are and then considering these factors at three levels of economic activity—the country, local, and consumer levels. The hypotheses therefore test the effects of *economic development, business conditions, resource availability,* and *customer demandingness.*

Four Hypotheses

Economic Development. The study made reference to the standard United Nations classification of a country's stage of economic development, which turns on industrialization. The more industrialized a country is, the higher is its level of economic development. The UN classifies countries such as the United States, Japan, and the United Kingdom as developed or industrialized economies. Examples of industrializing or developing countries are Brazil, China, and Indonesia. The UN's distinctions match the division of countries into those that belong to the Organization for Economic Co-operation and Development(OECD), that is, the developed nations, and those that do not, the developing nations.

Brands are challenged in developing economies to offer their products at the lowest possible cost to customers, who typically have low earning and buying power. This seems to favor a competitor orientation so as to achieve a cost advantage. By contrast, developed countries typically feature highly segmented customers with differentiated needs and satisfactions and considerable buying power as well as a broader and more complex competitive set. This favors a customer orientation both because meeting customer needs under such conditions means targeting products to narrower segments and because in an environment with more competitors it is more costly to allocate a brand's resources to gather information about those competitors. These considerations generated the hypothesis that the more developed an economy is, the stronger should be the effect of a customer orientation on a brand's performance. By contrast, the less developed an economy is, the stronger should be the effect of a competitor orientation.

Local Business Conditions. Local business conditions, which vary widely around the world, include the quality of the infrastructure, the political environment, the availability of value chain partners, and customs and culture. Political instability, an unfamiliar legal system, and the absence of markets for strategic factors of production create poor local business conditions. Under such circumstances, a brand will often need to develop relationships based largely on personal ties and informal networks of acquaintances to make connections with local politicians and business leaders and thereby secure the necessary institutional support.[6] This favors a competitor orientation because a brand is more likely to establish its own connections to institutional supports when it knows how and with whom its competitors do business. The hypothesis this observation yields is that the poorer the local business conditions, the weaker should be the effect of a customer orientation on brand performance. By the same token, the poorer the local business conditions, the stronger should be the effect of a competitor orientation.

Resource Availability. Developing economies often lack such important resources as qualified employees, managerial talent, reliable suppliers, and adequate investors. Hotel brands venturing into the global market therefore often contend to some degree with resource scarcity. Where resources exist, they might be difficult to acquire because of local constraints and dependencies.[7] This seems to favor a competitor orientation, because information about a brand's competitors in such a market might enable it to understand how other brands configure their value chains and identify resources and procurement approaches that are especially critical in that market. By contrast, developing a customer orientation in such a market seems less favorable, because without access to critical resources, customer information is of little use. Thus under these conditions a competitor orientation would seem to offer greater value than a customer orientation would. This observation yielded the hypothesis that the greater the resource availability, the stronger should be the effect of a customer orientation on brand performance. At the same time, the lower the resource availability, the stronger should be the effect of a competitor orientation.

Customer Demandingness. Finally, we considered customer demandingness as a factor regarding a customer versus a competitor orientation. Customer demandingness is the extent to which customers require superior quality or specific types of product and service performance to be satisfied with a brand's offerings. Demanding customers want greater benefits from the products and services they buy and are therefore more finely attuned to subtle differences within a product category. A brand facing a market featuring high levels of customer demandingness needs to tailor its offerings to highly specific and heterogeneous customer demands. Here a customer orientation would seem to confer greater value on a brand than a competitor orientation would. With an effectively established customer orientation, a brand in such a market can understand how to satisfy highly specific, specialized customer requirements and also anticipate changing requirements. By contrast, a competitor orientation, while perhaps still offering some value to a brand in such a market, is less likely to return as much value as a customer orientation would. A brand operating with a competitor orientation will find it tempting to emulate what it perceives as successful rivals without critically evaluating their marketing strategies. These considerations yielded the hypothesis that the more demanding the customers, the stronger should be the effect of a customer orientation on brand performance. Conversely, the less demanding the customers, the weaker should be the effect of a competitor orientation.

The Study

SAMPLE

The study was based on a survey of 185 hotel general and senior managers in fifty-six countries (twenty-six OECD and thirty non-OECD nations) across six continents, covering a variety of local market conditions. The global sweep and complexity of the sample enabled the study to yield both theoretical and practical implications. The average hotel in the sample offered 365 rooms and had been operating for twenty-three years.

MEASURES

Most of the measures were adopted from previous work, following a review of relevant literature and informal discussions with industry practitioners, although some were adopted specifically for this study. The measures included (1) *market orientation* (comprising customer orientation and competitor orientation, with interfunctional coordination included as a control variable); (2) *organizational performance* (comprising occupancy, gross operating profit, and market share); (3) *economic development* (based on OECD classification, with OECD members coded as developed markets and non-OECD members as developing markets); and (4) *local market environment* (comprising customer demandingness, local business conditions, resource availability, and availability of local investors). Statistical tests confirmed the validity and reliability of these measures.

The control variables included in the study were economic growth, government restrictions, entry barriers, competitive intensity, brand size, and innovation orientation. The study also analyzed the measures for possible interaction effects.

Results

The results of the study show that, as expected, a customer orientation has a greater effect on hotels' performance than does a competitor orientation, as the main effect of a customer orientation on performance was generally statistically positive and significant, whereas the effects of a competitor orientation and interfunctional coordination were insignificant across the board.[8] These results indicate that, by and large, the more developed a market's economy is, the more effective is a customer orientation. Conversely, a competitor orientation works better in a developing economy.

Almost all the hypotheses tested in the study were confirmed by the results. Confirmation was achieved for both hypotheses pertaining to economic development, both pertaining to local business conditions, both pertaining to resource availability, and one of the two pertaining to customer demandingness. Regarding the effects of a customer versus a competitor orientation on performance as related to economic development, a customer orientation was positively related to OECD membership, while a competitor orientation was negatively related to such membership. Regarding the possible effects as related to local business conditions, there was a strong positive relationship between good local business conditions and a customer orientation, but a negative relationship between competitor orientation and good local business conditions. Regarding effects related to resource and investor availability, there was a positive relationship between a customer orientation and a resource-rich environment but a negative relationship with a competitor orientation. Finally, for effects related to customer demandingness, the results were mixed. There was a positive relationship between a customer orientation and high customer demandingness, but there was no significant correlation with a competitor orientation, disconfirming the hypothesis that a competitor orientation would hurt brand performance in a highly demanding market.

Additional, finer-grained tests further confirmed all the hypotheses except for the one pertaining to the effects of a competitor orientation on performance in a demanding market. A brand with a customer orientation can expect better performance in developed markets and in markets characterized by good local business conditions, high levels of resource availability, and highly demanding customers. Having a customer orientation does not, however, have a significant impact in markets where those environmental conditions do not exist. Conversely, as expected, a brand with a competitor orientation should expect better performance in precisely those markets where most of the conditions favorable to the impact of a customer orientation do not obtain—less developed markets characterized by poor local business conditions and resource scarcity.

Finally, it appears from these additional analyses that adopting a competitor orientation may actually be detrimental to a brand's performance in a market environment with high levels of investor availability (apart from other resources). This is likely because investors find markets in which other resources are already handy attractive, especially where the government's regulatory imprint is light or supportive and in other respects local business conditions are good. While a competitor orientation should support a brand in gaining access to resources, becoming familiar with government restrictions, and making useful connections with other businesses and parties in a local market, in a market in which these advantages are easily obtained a brand's investment in a competitor orientation may simply not be cost effective.

Actionable Insights

The study presented in this chapter used the global hotel market, with its wide range of environmental conditions, to contribute to our theoretical understanding of a market orientation. In particular, the results support the contingency approach to the study of market orientation, as the effectiveness of such a strategic posture (and internal business culture) varies with differences in environmental factors.

Consider first the relative level of development within which a brand will have to operate as it moves into a foreign country. Here the results are clear. A brand moving into a developed or OECD market can achieve a competitive advantage if it establishes a customer orientation. On the other hand, a brand moving into a developing or non-OECD market should establish a competitor orientation. These two components of a market orientation both yield valuable information that, in keeping with the goals of such an orientation, should be disseminated throughout an organization to inform the policies and practices of all relevant departments. But the type of information that is typically provided through a customer orientation seems not to benefit a brand in a non-OECD country, while the reverse is true for the type of information that is typically provided through a competitor orientation.

Considering the local market level, our results confirm the conventional wisdom that markets in developed countries feature better business conditions than those of their counterparts in developing countries. Accordingly, brands moving into markets characterized by good local business conditions should orient themselves toward learning about and responding to customer needs, while brands moving into markets characterized by poor local business conditions should orient themselves toward learning how their key competitors operate in such markets. In a stable market a brand does not need specialized knowledge about idiosyncratic local customs or important local agents to succeed where these elements of success are readily available. In developing markets a brand cannot acquire the resources or institutional support that it needs on the basis of information about the customer base.

Finally, then, a brand entering a market characterized by a highly demanding customer base, again often a correlate of a highly developed economy, should establish a customer orientation, especially one that is attuned to indications of future demand. Such a strategic orientation should enable a brand operating in a developed economy to anticipate how its customers might respond to future offerings in terms of amenities and price points. Here, a competitor orientation perhaps will not hurt performance directly, but it will draw corporate resources away from collecting and disseminating the type of customer intelligence needed in such a market. If your customers are highly demanding, you had better find out what they want now and what they'll want tomorrow.

---

1 See, in particular, Ajay K. Kohli and Bernard Jaworski, "Market Orientation: The Construct, Research Propositions, and Managerial Implications," *Journal of Marketing* 54, no. 2 (1990): 1–18; and John C. Narver and Stanley F. Slater, "The Effect of a Market Orientation on Business Profitability," *Journal of Marketing* 54, no. 4 (1990): 20–35.

2 Narver and Slater, "The Effect of a Market Orientation," 21–22.

3 Ibid., 21.

4 See John Fahy, Graham Hooley, Tony Cox, Jozsef Bcracs, Krzysztof Fonfara, and Boris Snoj, "The Development and Impact of Marketing Capabilities in Central Europe," *Journal of International Business Studies* 31, no. 1 (2000): 63–81.

5 George S. Day and Robin Wensley, "Assessing Advantage," *Journal of Marketing* 52, no. 2 (1988): 1–20.

6 See, for example, Mike W. Peng and Peggy Sue Heath, "The Growth of the Firm in Planned Economies in Transition: Institutions, Organizations, and Strategic Choice," *Academy of Management Review* 21, no. 2 (1996): 492–528; Mike W. Peng and Y. Luo, "Managerial Ties and Firm Performance in a Transition Economy: The Nature of a Micro-Macro Link," *Academy of Management Journal* 43, no. 3 (2000): 486–501.

7 See Jeffrey Pfeffer and Gerald R. Salancik, *The External Control of Organizations: A Resource Dependence Perspective* (New York: Harper and Row, 1978).

8 See George S. Day and P. Nedungadi, "Managerial Representations of Competitive Advantage," *Journal of Marketing* 58, no. 2 (1994): 31–44.

CASE STUDY TWO

Ritz-Carlton Bali

The business model under which many hotels operate, in which a property owner uses a management contract to engage a hotel brand to run its facility, has not always worked smoothly, because of the complexities involved in the use by the property of the brand's resources and name. Since the early 1990s, however, a series of court cases in which property owners have litigated to protect their interests has gradually clarified the legal obligations that a hotel property manager incurs under such a contract.[1]

A hotel management contract ideally benefits both the property owner and the operating company. The owner benefits from the value added to the property by the prestige, marketing skill, and good management of the operator. The operator has a profitable revenue source whereby the capitalization is provided by the owner. Tensions arise between owner and operator when there are perceived conflicts of interest or when the operator stresses brand standards (higher operating costs) while the owner prefers reducing the bottom line. When such tensions arise, the details of hotel management contract terms matter.

The fog surrounding such issues is clearing. Following important legal cases of the 1990s, a recently adjudicated case seems to have made it apparent that hotel companies should view their relationships with property owners with whom they contract to manage properties as a form of *agency*. This means that a management contract applies within a set of constraints that can supersede its specific terms because the law recognizes specific fiduciary and other rights pertaining to any entity that hires an agent to represent its interests. This chapter reviews a case that unfolded recently on the island of Bali involving the Marriott Corporation's Ritz-Carlton brand and a venture into the hotel business by the high-end Italian jewelry brand Bulgari SpA. The case played out against important brand-related trends. The chapter reviews highlights of the case and summarizes the implications of these developments for brand management.

In the case of *KMS v. Ritz-Carlton,* P. T. Karang Mas Sejahtera (KMS) was the owner of the Ritz-Carlton Bali Resort and Spa, a luxury property managed by Ritz-Carlton.[2] Ritz-Carlton is a subsidiary of Marriott International Inc. KMS sued Marriott and Ritz-Carlton because the latter, in partnership with Bulgari, opened a luxury resort and spa in Bali, the same market in which KMS operated the Ritz-Carlton Bali. KMS claimed that this action violated its management contract with Ritz-Carlton; the outcome of the case affirmed this claim and was another instance in which the courts have applied agency law to disputes involving management contracts. The case involves several issues pertaining to brand practices and brand rights.

Brand Rights, Co-branding, and Brand Extension

BRAND RELATIONSHIPS INVOLVED
IN *KMS v. RITZ-CARLTON*

A brand is a trademark or, when the brand applies to an entire firm, a trade name. Practically, however, a brand is an "intangible" or abstract concept in the minds of consumers, carrying important implications for consumer buying decisions.[3] From a marketing standpoint, the purpose of a brand is to attract consumers to buy a good or service by associating that good or service with an expectation that it will satisfy the consumer's purpose in entering a marketplace.

There are over three hundred hotel brands in the United States and nearly five hundred worldwide. There are not, of course, this many hotel *companies*—through *brand extension* and *co-branding* many hotel brands are operated by individual hotel companies. Marriott, for example, includes several brands among its subsidiaries, including such familiar names as Courtyard by Marriott, Renaissance Hotels and Resorts, Fairfield Inns by Marriott, and, of course, Ritz-Carlton. To this list we should add Bulgari Hotels and Resorts, which is affiliated with Marriott through its co-branding partnership with Ritz-Carlton. The association between Ritz-Carlton and Bulgari is the basis of the lawsuit. We shall see that Marriott publicized this relationship sufficiently to establish that the Bulgari Bali involved a co-branding partnership between Bulgari and Ritz-Carlton that violated the brand rights of the Ritz-Carlton Bali.

BRAND RIGHTS

When one company buys another with a recognizable brand name, the buying company often also purchases the right to use that brand in marketing its own products as well as already branded products. Hotel management contracts typically involve brand rights because hotel property owners engage with hotel management companies like Ritz-Carlton to benefit from name recognition and a favorable brand image. The brand rights in such a case typically remain in force for the duration of the contract and apply to a specified territory within which the management firm or agent may not operate a comparable property bearing the same brand. This has been expressed in the literature as the "right to a reasonable, restrictive (non-compete) covenant."[4] Such a covenant expressly acknowledges a right against competition that arises automatically under agency law.

Branded hotel operating companies by their very nature seek growth, which means situating as many properties as possible in as many markets as possible. When managers attempt to move multiple brands into a market, the implications for other properties depend on how the brands are positioned. After all, there is little resemblance between, say, a Ritz-Carlton and a Fairfield Inn. But the potential for conflict by introducing multiple brands within one market is obvious.[5]

Brand Management Issues Pertaining to *KMS* v. *Ritz-Carlton*

The creation of the Bulgari Hotels and Resorts brand is an example of brand extension, extending both the Bulgari brand (into the hotel business) and the Ritz-Carlton brand (into a new line of luxury properties). From a marketing standpoint, when one entity's brand management strategies adversely affect another entity's market position, *brand dilution* results. Whether this is a case of brand dilution depends crucially on the relationship between Ritz-Carlton and Bulgari in the Bali market, where it affects the Ritz-Carlton Bali. It seems to be a case of co-branding, however, because it is a marriage of Ritz-Carlton's expertise in the development, marketing, and management of luxury hotel properties with Bulgari's expertise in design and luxury product marketing. Bulgari provides the design features of its hotel properties, while Ritz-Carlton provides the approach to managing the facilities and molding the personnel and services into a set of viable offerings that suggest to the consumer that to stay at a Bulgari hotel is to experience the ultimate in luxurious, personalized service and amenities.

The problem in the Bali case was that there was already a Ritz-Carlton in Bali. The Bulgari property therefore posed a threat to the Ritz-Carlton Bali owned by KMS, which, however strong its reputation, would now face a competitor in its local market. To be sure, the name Ritz-Carlton rarely occurs in the consumer-facing communications or facilities of Bulgari Hotels and Resorts (although the initial marketing campaigns of Marriott, Ritz-Carlton, and Bulgari prominently featured Ritz-Carlton's role). In this case, co-branding in the form of the Bulgari Bali might dilute the brand equity that the Ritz-Carlton Bali enjoyed through its relationship with Ritz-Carlton.

The Case

KMS v. RITZ-CARLTON: ONE COMPANY, TWO LUXURY BRANDS IN PARTNERSHIP

When Marriott entered into its partnership with Bulgari in 2001, Ritz-Carlton was the natural choice to help develop, market, and manage the new properties. With Ritz-Carlton's exclusive brand image conveying the ultimate quality in hotel service and amenities and Bulgari's exclusive brand image conveying the ultimate style in jewelry and accessories, the new Bulgari Hotels and Resorts promised to set a new standard of luxury and haute couture in the hotel industry. With both brands, Ritz-Carlton and Bulgari, the Marriott brand itself would remain in the background.

Yet the Bulgari initiative would involve the Ritz-Carlton brand and the question became, Did Marriott, in arranging for Ritz-Carlton to help develop, market, and manage the Bulgari hotel properties, violate the brand rights that KMS had acquired through its management contract with Ritz-Carlton? The answer, according to the jury, was an emphatic yes. The lawsuit that was filed on behalf of KMS alleged that it violated both territorial and other brand rights pertaining to its use of the Ritz-Carlton name, and we now consider the merits of that case in some detail. The jury also found that Ritz-Carlton had committed a material breach of the management agreement, which permitted KMS to immediately terminate its contract with Ritz-Carlton.

THE ARGUMENTS

Ritz-Carlton argued that its role in the operation of the Bulgari hotels did not involve Ritz-Carlton brand rights, because the Bulgari brand is strong enough to stand on its own, and neither of the existing Bulgari hotel properties bore the Ritz-Carlton name or logo on its premises. In whatever way the Ritz-Carlton name might have been used to promote these new hotels, there was nothing that it could add to the cachet of the Bulgari name, which, if anything, was positioned to provide an even more exclusive level of luxury and style. Moreover, according to the defense, its contract with KMS effectively made Ritz-Carlton an independent contractor, able to use its name freely for its own purposes.

To see why Ritz-Carlton lost its arguments, consider the language, below, from the management contract between KMS and Ritz-Carlton. KMS argued that building the Bulgari Bali only about five kilometers from the Ritz-Carlton Bali violated clause 2.7 of the contract, which provided the following protection against the potential competitive disadvantage of another Ritz-Carlton-operated hotel in the Bali market:

2.7 Territorial Restriction

(a) From and after the [...] Commencement Date while this agreement shall be in effect, Operator [Ritz-Carlton] shall not, without prior approval of Owner [KMS] [...] open another hotel using the Ritz-Carlton rights within the Island of Bali, Indonesia [...].

This clearly is the equivalent of a radius clause in this management contract. In fact, the agreement prohibited Ritz-Carlton from managing a comparable hotel property on Bali for a ten-year period that would end in 2014, after which it provided for an approximately forty-five-kilometer radius within which Ritz-Carlton was not to operate such a hotel. The critical phrase in this clause is, however, "Ritz-Carlton rights." Apparently Marriott's determination to jump on a worldwide marketing strategy bandwagon persuaded it to neglect the fact that by situating the new property on Bali it risked violating KMS's contract with Ritz-Carlton.[6] Marriott ignored the potential conflict with the Ritz-Carlton Bali because the new property would not be called a Ritz-Carlton. KMS was able to convince the jury, however, that the radius clause applied in this case because the manner in which the Bulgari was developed, managed, and marketed violated those brand rights acquired by KMS. The Ritz-Carlton brand rights include

(i) the names and marks "Ritz-Carlton"; (ii) the Ritz-Carlton logo attached hereto as Exhibit B; and (iii) all other words, trademarks, indicia of origin, slogans and designs...used or registered by Ritz-Carlton or any of its Affiliates and which are used to identify or are otherwise used in connection with Ritz-Carlton Chain hotels...—all of the foregoing being indicative of the renowned Ritz-Carlton mystique, programs, processes, procedures, and systems.

In arguing that the relationship between Ritz-Carlton and Bulgari, in particular with respect to the Bulgari hotel in Bali, violated these rights, KMS focused its testimony on the intangible assets that Ritz-Carlton provided. In an exchange of testimony between expert witnesses for both sides, a witness for Ritz-Carlton argued that, because the Bulgari Bali did not publicly display the Ritz-Carlton name or logo on its physical, tangible assets, Ritz-Carlton had not violated KMS's brand rights. In rebutting this testimony, an expert witness for KMS argued that the intangible attributes "are the very attributes underlying the Ritz-Carlton rights in this case."[7] Indeed, KMS was able to show that the Bulgari Bali project publicly involved not only explicit references to Ritz-Carlton as a "partner" with Bulgari in various media, but more specifically that it involved many elements of the list of intangibles in the above-quoted brand rights clause of the management contract. For its part, Ritz-Carlton argued that because it was an independent contractor with KMS it bore no responsibility for any fiduciary duties owed to KMS under agency law.

In the end, abundant evidence and testimony established that, in marketing terms, Marriott and Ritz-Carlton had arranged a co-branding partnership between Bulgari and Ritz-Carlton. In reference to the above-quoted brand rights clause of the management contract, Marriott was using the Ritz-Carlton name to market the new venture in the industry as well as Ritz-Carlton managerial expertise to manage the property. Expert testimony established this proposition to the satisfaction of the jury. In particular, it was shown that, not only did the name Ritz-Carlton as well as references to it as Bulgari's "partner" appear on various websites and other media available publicly, but Bulgari would be using Ritz-Carlton's staff training and career development processes, central reservation system, and incentive system for travel agents and group travel brokers as well as a Ritz-Carlton booth at a trade fair.

Clearly, Bulgari coveted Ritz-Carlton's hotel management cachet to legitimize its hotel venture. An expert witness argued that co-branding was an explicit part of the strategy, quoting Bulgari CEO Francesco Trapani: "In lodging, the brand is becoming more important. You're happier if you're able to say, 'I went to a brand that's considered prestigious.'" Adding, "We could not afford to be unsuccessful," Trapani further indicated the brand value that

Bulgari perceived in a partnership with Ritz-Carlton. As the witness suggested, "Mr. Trapani feels that customers need to be convinced that they would not be disappointed at a Bulgari hotel because Bulgari hotels had the Ritz-Carlton hospitality engine under its hood."[8]

THE DECISION

On January 25, 2008, the jury handed down its decision to assess compensatory and punitive damages and to permit KMS to terminate its management contract with Ritz-Carlton.[9] After the case was dismissed, KMS terminated its management agreement with Ritz-Carlton, contracting with another management company, the West Paces Hotel Group, and rebranding its Bali property to become the Ayana Resort and Spa in 2009.

Ritz-Carlton's claims that the Bulgari brand name needed no help from Ritz-Carlton lacked credibility. KMS was able to convince the jury that Marriott's exploiting the cachet of the Ritz-Carlton brand posed a competitive threat to KMS in violation of its fiduciary duties—and contractual arrangement—with Ritz-Carlton. In its so doing, the jury also found the argument based on Ritz-Carlton's contractual status as an independent contractor unconvincing, instead finding that Ritz-Carlton did, after all, owe to KMS a range of fiduciary duties that included not competing with another property it was operating.

Actionable Insights

KMS v. Ritz-Carlton was almost immediately hailed as an important case, confirming yet again the applicability of agency law to hotel management contracts, thereby providing legal recourse against perceived violations of fiduciary duties associated with agency law, even if a given contract might seem not to impose such duties explicitly. No longer can a hotel management company, no matter the strength and scope of its corporate resources, successfully defend itself on the grounds that it acts as an independent contractor when arranging to manage hotel properties, or that contractual clauses explicitly render its agency power revocable. This case decisively demonstrates that developers and property owners have achieved a much stronger position relative to that of hotel management companies, a position that is now recognized by the courts.

In this era of profligate brand extension in industry after industry, these rulings should provide to prospective hotel property owners some measure of confidence that, when they enter busy hotel markets with multiple brand extensions and co-branded operations, they are protected against same-brand competition in their respective competitive sets and market segments. It should encourage them to raise challenges to potential difficulties by reminding hotel managers that they owe to property owners a set of duties, which may well supersede specific rights that are included in contractual language. Fiduciary responsibilities, including loyalty and not competing with existing properties, apply regardless of specific contractual terms. Now property owners can more easily include in management contracts explicit terms that reflect these duties, and managers can no longer assume that duties that are not explicit in contracts do not apply. This should reduce the incidence of lawsuits.

These rulings should also cause hotel management companies with lengthy brand portfolios to expand into new markets much more carefully than they may have in the past. It can no longer be assumed that market expansion decisions involve only a simple calculation weighing minor settlement fees against prospective market gains. In the case discussed in this chapter, it is likely that the allure of a partnership between Bulgari and Ritz-Carlton was too powerful to pass up. Perhaps the largest hotel management companies will continue to accept such lawsuits as a cost of doing business. It seems likely, though, that they will take much greater care to avoid such same-brand conflicts in the future.

Alternatively, hotel firms might be more willing to assume the burdens of property ownership in some markets, since independent property owners seem now to have the upper hand. That will always depend in particular cases on detailed cost and profitability analyses, but these companies now realize that their efforts to build brand equity will be more difficult because they cannot do so without simultaneously promoting and preserving the rights of property owners.

One particular change in business practice that can be attributed to the case is that operating agreements are now being negotiated separately from brand rights, in separate documents, each with its own fee structure. This will likely become a permanent change in modus operandi for the negotiation and administration of hotel management contracts by branded hotel management companies.

---

1 The most important of these were *Robert E. Woolley et al. v. Embassy Suites, Inc. et al.* (1991), *Pacific Landmark Hotel, Ltd. v. Marriott Hotels, Inc.* (1993), *Government Guarantee Fund of the Republic of Finland v. Hyatt Corporation* (1996, 1998), and *2660 Woodley Road Joint Venture v. ITT Sheraton Corporation* (1998, 1999). These cases have had the cumulative effect, reflected in the disposition

of *KMS v. Ritz-Carlton,* of clarifying (and apparently restricting) the rights of companies operating hotel properties under management contracts.

2 The legal case is known officially as P. T. Karang Mas Sejahtera v. The Ritz-Carlton Hotel Company, LLC (Civil Action No.: 8:05-cv-00787-PJM).

3 Kevin Lane Keller, *Strategic Brand Management: Building, Measuring, and Managing Brand Equity,* 3rd ed. (Upper Saddle River, NJ: Prentice-Hall, 2008), 10.

4 Chad Crandell, Kristie Dickinson, and Fern Kanter, "Negotiating the Hotel Management Contract," in *Hotel Asset Management: Principles and Practices,* ed. Paul Beals and Greg Denton, 85–104 (Lansing, MI: Educational Institute of the American Hotel Motel and Lodging Association, 2003).

5 For more on this topic, see Jon M. McCarthy and Lori E. Raleigh, "Evaluating Franchise and Chain Affiliation Programs," in Beals and Denton, *Hotel Asset Management.*

6 Similar partnerships have included Baccarat Hotels and Resorts, a partnership between Starwood Capital and Baccarat Crystal, and Armani Hotels and Resorts, a partnership between Emaar Hotels and Resorts LLC and Giorgio Armani SpA. Donatella Versace has a hotel property (but not yet a chain), the Palazzo Versace, in Australia, with another opening in Dubai.

7 Chekitan S. Dev, Expert Report, "Rebuttals to the Critiques of My Opinions by: Dr. Jeffery Alan Durbin and Mr. Roger Cline," in Civil Action No 8:05-cv-00787-PJM, *P. T. Karang Mas Sejahtera,* Plaintiff, *v. Marriott International, Inc.,* et al., Defendants, 6.

8 Ibid., 10.

9 The case was decided under the laws of the State of Georgia, pursuant to a clause in the parties' operating agreement.

▶ PART THREE ◀

STRATEGIC BRANDING

CHAPTER SEVEN

Brand Equity

B uilding a strong brand, or *brand equity*, drives business success. This chapter examines brand equity in the hotel industry and demonstrates a method
for measuring it. The objective of the exercise is to offer a diagnostic and decision-making tool to CEOs and top managers of hotel companies that could
help them maximize brand value. In the absence of real-life examples of brand
equity measurement, the chapter sketches a hypothetical but realistic demonstration of how a proposed brand equity index was developed and can be used
to assess a brand's strength over time and in relation to its competitive set.

Brand equity helps differentiate a product, allowing brand owners to charge
a premium and foster customer loyalty.[1] What, however, is a brand? In the
simplest terms it is a name, a logo, a symbol, an identity, or a trademark. Beyond that notion is the complex idea that a brand embodies all that a business
stands for. In its most complex incarnation, a brand is a hallmark of quality, a
promise or assurance to buyers, a set of associations or expectations, a perception or an image that persuades customers to purchase a brand's products. As
such a brand becomes a symbol that connects a company or its products with
its customers in an ongoing relationship and represents the entire "product
personality."[2]

A brand's strength develops over time. Building a strong brand is difficult
and costly, given the rapid proliferation of new brands, dramatic increases in
media costs, the more extensive and aggressive use of promotions by established firms, and the cost and difficulty of obtaining distribution.[3] Some estimates put the cost of creating a brand at around $150 million.[4] Clearly, only
effective brand management can maximize shareholder value, and a properly
positioned and effectively managed brand can deter new brand entry.[5] Conversely, poorly managed brands are often targeted by new brand entries. To

maintain its competitive advantage against existing and potential competitors, a brand needs an effective strategy to build and maintain brand equity.

Customers are the ultimate arbiters of brand equity and shareholder value because they generate all cash flows and profits.[6] Brand equity is therefore defined by repeat purchases caused by brand use satisfaction, perceived superior value, and a felt preference or loyalty for a brand. The framework presented in the following sections is an attempt to capture the essence of this notion by describing a hypothetical customer centric index of hotel brand equity measured over time and against competitors.

Hotel Brand Equity

Hotel chains represent a classic application of brand strategy. Brands allow hotels and hotel chains to identify and differentiate themselves quickly in the minds of customers. A brand symbolizes the essence of customer perceptions of a hotel, its products, and its services.[7] In this context, brand equity resides in the favorable or unfavorable attitudes and perceptions that are formed by and influence customers. Good experiences with a hotel brand build brand equity, while bad experiences erode it. Yet customers need no firsthand experience with a brand to form an impression of it: brand equity is formed among nonusers by exposure to media messages or word of mouth.

Why Measure Brand Equity?

Insofar as growing brand equity drives future business success, there is an incentive to quantify and measure such equity.[8] For one thing, a measure of brand equity would provide a single, critical gauge of customer feedback. If we could measure brand recognition or awareness, brand perception, and overall customer satisfaction with a brand's performance, we could determine whether the brand's equity was growing, declining, or stagnating. Moreover, tracked over time, a brand equity measure would reflect brand strength against that of competitors. Finally, a brand equity measure would reveal the impact of a brand's own marketing mix on customers, delineating the evolution of the brand's equity.

Measuring Hotel Brand Equity

Here we derive brand equity from a range of customer satisfaction criteria. A hotel will have strong brand equity when a large number of customers perceive it favorably and behave accordingly. High equity means high customer satisfaction, brand preference, and loyalty; high guest retention; high market share; a price premium; high profits; and, finally, good shareholder value. One could say that brand equity is the sum of all net favorable or positive ratings paid into a brand's equity account.

We measure a hotel brand's equity via multifaceted customer ratings. Using customer research data from brand awareness and brand usage (A&U) studies, a hotel brand can collect and analyze data from a national panel consisting of over one hundred thousand households that mirror the U.S. population. Random samples can be drawn from such a panel to conduct A&U and guest satisfaction tracking studies. We present hypothetical findings from such surveys to demonstrate the utility of measuring brand equity as a function of customer perceptions, attitudes, use, and satisfaction.

On the approach proposed in this chapter, the first step in computing brand equity is quantifying customer satisfaction ratings of five key brand attributes that constitute, respectively, our key indicators—brand performance and brand awareness. Brand performance is measured by overall satisfaction with product and service, return intent, price-value perception, and brand preference, while brand awareness is measured by brand recall. Based on a classification of these customer ratings for a specific brand and its principal competitors, the resulting performance and awareness indices can be combined to develop a unified measure, the brand equity index.

TRACKING PERCEPTIONS

To measure brand equity, a simple spreadsheet-based application has been developed under the trademarked name BrandTracker, which converts the quantitative customer ratings first into performance and awareness indices and then into a brand equity index. This computational model tracks customer brand perceptions over time, supports remedial marketing strategies, measures the effects of remedial actions, and tracks competitor brand equity. BrandTracker can be used to gauge favorable customer perception of a hotel brand, representing the strength of such a brand in terms of satisfaction, return intent, price-value, and preference. This system allows a brand manager to compare perceptions of his or her brand with those of competing brands, providing a benchmark for analyzing customer preference trends over time. Changes over time or in relation to other brands could suggest diagnostic questions supporting the brand manager's efforts to embrace opportunities or address challenges.

Remedial Marketing

The diagnostic questions, in turn, can be used to identify problems that require remedial action in marketing or operational areas. The brand equity index can reveal an area needing additional investigation and makes it possible to address multifaceted problems. If the index shows a decline in return intent, for example, this could be due to such diverse factors as poor guest service, dated guest rooms, or an outdated guest-preference program. Similarly, a downward trend in awareness would recommend a review of advertising strategy.

Measuring Effectiveness and Monitoring Competitors

It is easy to track the effectiveness of such remedial actions after implementation by using the same BrandTracker model for the following year or for earlier years. Also, the brand awareness, brand performance, and brand equity measures reveal changes in competing brands' relative positions.

Classifying Brand Types

The BrandTracker model can be used to classify the hotel brands into four categories based on high or low awareness plotted against high or low performance. The categories are *brand champions* (high performance, high awareness), *rising brands* (high performance, low awareness), *troubled brands* (low performance, high awareness), and *weak brands* (low on both indices).

Brand Champions

Hotel brands that rate high in both awareness and performance are the industry leaders or brand champions. Customers recall these brands well and rate their performance above those of other brands. Brand champions should be able to command strong occupancies and room rates, thus garnering strong profits.

Rising Brands

Rising brands have strong customer followings but not widespread awareness, most likely as a result of their short history in the marketplace. Some rising brands have not yet grown beyond a particular region or submarket to generate nationwide exposure.

Troubled Brands

BrandTracker classifies as troubled those brands that, although typically long established and thus recently high in top-of-mind and total awareness, no longer support the quality and consistency levels that customers expect. A brand can be troubled also by innovations that provide competitive advantage to other brands. Troubled brands have poor customer-satisfaction ratings and show declining top-of-mind awareness.

Weak Brands

Whether new or old, weak brands generate little differentiation in customers' minds, offer poor service delivery, or have weak brand strategies.

Applying BrandTracker

A hotel brand with high awareness, satisfaction, return intent, positive price-value perception, and brand preference ratings has, by definition, strong brand equity. BrandTracker expresses brand equity as percentages of customers' quantitative ratings of satisfaction and other positive ratings. These percentages are then converted into the two indices of brand performance and awareness.

This can be demonstrated by developing a database for a hypothetical set of competing hotel chains. The data will resemble those associated with real hotels to lend verisimilitude to the exercise. The hotel chains are designated by invented names—Crawford Inn, Davis Inn, Hamilton Inn, Harrison Inn, Parker Inn, and Signet Inn (it would be pure coincidence if any is the name of an actual chain or hotel).

With indexing, the BrandTracker model can be used to compare brand equity among competing brands and also to track equity values over time. The mean for the hypothetical competitive set is an index of 100 for performance and awareness, which then becomes the point of reference for measuring equity. A score of less than 100 is below average, while a score of, say, 110, is above average.

The following steps for computing the brand awareness and brand performance indices generate the single comprehensive brand equity index.

Step 1: Cull ratings data on guest satisfaction, return intent, and price-value performance for each brand from the lodger panel. Note users' brand preferences from the A&U studies to calculate the performance index. A brand's top-of-mind recall and awareness data are also taken from A&U studies.

Step 2: For each brand, add the percentages pertaining to the four performance indicator ratings to arrive at total performance points.

Step 3: Calculate the mean performance points for each brand by dividing the total points by four, which is the number of attributes for the performance indicator. This is called the Mean Performance Indicator. The Brand Performance Index is calculated by indexing the Mean Performance Indicator scores across all the brands—the average being indexed at 100. Each brand's specific performance index is compared with this index-100 value to establish its particular index value (and place in the typology).

Step 4: Since there is just one attribute for awareness, no further calculation is necessary to find its mean. Awareness scores are averaged across all brands and indexed to 100. Each brand's specific awareness index is compared with this index-100 value to establish its particular index value (and place in the typology).

Step 5: Next, compare the performance and awareness indices for each brand to show where each stands relative to the others and which category (champion, rising, troubled, or weak) it occupies.

Step 6: Finally, compute the brand equity index by combining the awareness and performance indexes. To produce a single index number, the awareness index is weighted by 20 percent and performance by 80 percent. This weighting acknowledges that the awareness index involves one criterion while the performance index involves four.

Test Case

Suppose now we imagine developing an "actual" lodger panel and A&U data for "Signet Inn" and its competing midmarket brands based on ratios similar to those found in the industry. That is, although the figures inputted into BrandTracker are arbitrary, they are also realistic. What follows is an analysis of the resulting indices.

SIGNET INN

Suppose that Signet has a brand equity index of 103, which is below Hamilton's index of 115. Let's say this is primarily a result of Signet's much lower performance index (113 compared with Hamilton's 120), which is caused by the high proportion (50 percent) of business travelers using the Hamilton brand who selected it as their brand of first choice. Let's say that Signet was chosen by only 29 percent.

Similarly, imagine that Signet's awareness index, 65, is not only below Hamilton's (at 91), but also well below Harrison's (239). As a much older brand, Harrison shows strong top-of-mind brand awareness. While Signet would seem to need awareness-building initiatives, we can also imagine that it shows a positive performance index, putting it ahead of Harrison Inn and all other brands except Hamilton. In particular, let's say that Signet leads Hamilton in return intent and price-value perception, while nearly equaling it in guest satisfaction.

Since Signet is driven by strong performance ratings and a weak brand awareness level among customers, we should classify it as a rising brand. Strong brand awareness could make it a brand champion.

The strategic significance of all this from Signet Inn's perspective is twofold. First, Signet has to build brand awareness as a top priority. Advertising heavily to its target audience could help. Second, the chain must improve and sustain performance to become the brand of choice. Somehow its customers' high return intent is not translated into being chosen ahead of Hamilton. Perhaps a well-designed guest recognition program would improve the situation.

SIGNET'S COMPETITORS

Harrison Inn. Given our arbitrary figures, Harrison Inn leads all others in the brand equity index, yet we can imagine that Harrison Inn is a troubled brand. It has the highest brand recall, but its performance is below par. Its brand equity is driven mainly by top-of-mind brand recall.

Indeed, in our hypothetical example Harrison Inn leads all brands in top-of-mind awareness with 239 index points. Let's say the closest competitor is Parker Inn, trailing Harrison by over 100 points. Suppose, on the other hand, that Harrison's brand performance index of 98 is below that of Hamilton, Davis, and Signet. Here it is possible that Harrison Inn has traditionally spent heavily on media advertising to sustain high awareness and is widely distributed, but has developed a reputation for service delivery inconsistency and has a portfolio containing many tired properties. The remedy seems to lie in improving hotel operations and capital spending to refurbish its older hotels. Harrison Inn's CEO and brand manager must undertake a major strategic task.

Crawford Inn. Let's suppose this is a weak brand as a result of low brand equity (87) and awareness (61). Such figures almost certainly reflect performance weakness by most customercentric measures (we can make an exception for price-value perception if we assume that Crawford pursues a low-room-rate strategy). If we imagine that Crawford represents one of the largest networks of hotels in the country, we see that it faces a daunting task to improve brand equity.

Hamilton Inn. Sticking with the brand equity index figure of 115 that we assigned to it, let's say that Hamilton leads the pack in brand performance with 120 points but lags behind Harrison Inn and Parker in top-of-mind brand recall. Its awareness index of 91 is 148 points below that of Harrison Inn. Perhaps this is because Hamilton has a narrower distribution base and is a much newer brand. It faces the challenge of building top-of-mind brand awareness via advertising. With higher awareness, Hamilton could become a brand champion, because it has a strong foundation in top performance.

Parker Inn. If we imagine that Parker is one of the older brands and has the second-highest brand awareness index at 104 but is the poorest performer (80) among the competitive set, we can see why this is a troubled brand. Its managers must work hard to prevent a slide from troubled brand to weak brand.

Davis Inn. Finally, let's say that Davis is a relatively new brand (which offers no food and beverage service) with the fourth-highest brand equity index. Let's give it a low awareness index of 35 points, resulting perhaps from its regional distribution, but a good performance index of 103 points. Thus, although it exhibits weakness in awareness, its strong performance index makes it a rising brand.

BrandTracker Lessons

Although we have considered only a hypothetical use of BrandTracker, the resulting brand equity analysis suggests that such an approach can reveal significant changes in a hotel marketplace with considerable brand strategy implications. Using this information, a brand manager can focus on why changes have occurred, what issues need to be addressed, and how to address these issues. This will not replace the traditional analysis of hotel brand performance in terms of occupancy, rate, and market share, but such statistics ignore the customercentric drivers of brand equity that are embodied in the BrandTracker analysis. Trend analysis based on it reveals market dynamics that other methodologies miss. For corporate leaders who watch equity markets, the message is simple—here is a factor that helps drive earnings.

Measuring brand equity benefits the following activities:

- Benchmarking brand equity evolution
- Setting measurable goals
- Tracking results
- Monitoring competitor performance
- Raising diagnostic questions
- Formulating marketing mix and operational strategies
- Improving performance through customer feedback

Brand Equity and Financial Performance

The result of this hypothetical analysis suggests that there is a positive correlation between brand equity and financial performance: A hotel with strong brand equity should command higher occupancy and rates, resulting in higher revenue per available room (RevPAR). As more customers are satisfied and see a positive price-value relationship, more will prefer the brand and more will return. This should translate into higher earnings.

Limitations

Although the hotel brand equity index conveniently summarizes customer information from lodger panels and A&U studies, its focus is brand perception across nationwide customer markets. It generates information regarding a specific hotel brand's image in the minds of a large population of customers. A chain smaller than, say, one hundred hotels or one that is not distributed nationwide may not appear in national panel surveys that provide data for the index. For smaller chains and individual brands, a separate panel would have to be conducted at the regional or destination level.

Although the index is not designed to replace other measurements such as yield, RevPAR, occupancy, room rate, or market share, it provides a heretofore unavailable tool for understanding a brand's equity.

1 David Aaker, *Managing Brand Equity* (New York: Free Press, 1991), 19–32.

2 See Lance Leuthesser, "Defining, Measuring, and Managing Brand Equity" (conference summary, Marketing Science Institute, Cambridge, MA, May 1988), 2; Kevin Lane Keller, "Conceptualizing, Measuring, and Managing Customer-Based Brand Equity" (working paper, Marketing Science Institute, Cambridge, MA, October 1991), 4; Rajendra K. Srivastava and Allan Shocker, "Brand Equity: A Perspective on Its Meaning and Measurement" (technical working paper, Marketing Science Institute, Cambridge, MA, October 1991), 5; Aaker, *Managing Brand Equity*, 7; and David Aaker, *Building Strong Brands* (New York: Free Press, 1996), 35.

3 David Aaker and Kevin Keller, "Consumer Evaluations of Brand Extensions," *Journal of Marketing* 54, no. 1 (1990): 27–41.

4 Edward Tauber, "Brand Leverage: Study for Growth in a Cost-Controlled World," *Journal of Advertising Research* 28, no. 4 (1988): 26–30.

5 Chekitan S. Dev, Michael Morgan, and Stowe Shoemaker, "A Positioning Analysis of Hotel Brands," *Cornell Hotel and Restaurant Administration Quarterly* 36, no. 6 (1995): 48–55.

6 David Arnold, *The Handbook of Brand Management* (Boston: Addison-Wesley, 1992), 142.

7 Kevin Keller, *Strategic Brand Management: Building, Measuring, and Managing Brand Equity* (New York: Prentice-Hall, 1997), 45–56.

8 Ibid., 372–79.

CHAPTER EIGHT

Brand Positioning

A hotel brand's unique selling proposition—the argument it makes to convince travelers to book its hotels instead of someone else's properties—is known as its *market position*. The position comprises the bundle of attributes that the hotel offers in an effort to meet guests' wants and needs. A brand's position can be viewed from two perspectives, that of the brand's management and that of the guests. The brand's management must have a firm concept of the hotel's intended position, and its promotional efforts must articulate not only what the brand offers but also how its offerings are distinct from those of other brands.

The Challenge

In the final analysis a brand's position is determined by its customers. A hotel company might offer a luxury-level package of services and amenities in an effort to attract business travelers, for instance. If the resulting room rate is higher than corporate travel managers are willing to pay, that brand is in reality not positioned for the bulk of business travelers. Instead it may attract only those who are price insensitive, or it may attract luxury-oriented leisure guests. Alternatively, if a hotel has positioned itself as the most effective and efficient conference hotel in the market, customers will expect their meetings to occur flawlessly. Should that not occur, the hotel's position—from the customer's point of view—will in reality be that of an average or below-average conference hotel or worse.

Customers' perceptions of a hotel brand's position can be subdivided into specific attributes. Such attributes can be depicted graphically on coordinate axes known as *perceptual maps*. Likewise, the position of an individual hotel or brand can be graphed, to allow a comparison of the brand's comparative position and to demonstrate changes in the brand's position over time. This chapter describes the development of such perceptual maps and suggests how to use them to show how a hotel brand's customers view the brand and help to determine its competitive set. The results that were mapped for the study were based on data drawn from surveys of travel managers and travel agents published over a three-year period.

POSITIONING BY ATTRIBUTE

Each hotel booking represents a purchase decision based on a customer's perception of the attributes represented by that brand. In the case of corporate travel offices, the customer is the person who makes the booking, regardless of who actually stays at the hotel. Those attributes are both tangible (the physical property) and intangible (services offered). Typical attributes might include a low price, a convenient location, a frequent-traveler program, or a helpful and courteous staff. The package of attributes offered by the brand constitutes its market position, which is usually viewed in relation to other brands' offerings. Brands with similar bundles of attributes are considered to be in the same competitive set.

The element of positioning that derives directly from the product's physical attributes and stated offerings is its *objective position*.[1] Such positioning distinguishes the Four Seasons, which offers luxury services, from Embassy Suites, which offers a suite priced to compete with conventional midprice brands,[2] and Motel 6, which offers consistent, low-priced rooms.

The other portion of the position is subjective, involving people's perceptions of a brand or individual property's intangible attributes. These can be experienced only during the hotel stay. As Robert Lewis succinctly put it, you cannot take a hotel stay home with you.[3] Most of a hotel's attributes are intangible, making it difficult for a customer to distinguish among competitive offerings. To enable customers to make that distinction, marketers attempt to establish a position using brand names and specific images or slogans that signify some of the intangible attributes. Lewis suggested that a successful position comprises three elements: it differentiates the brand, it "locates" the brand along specific benefit dimensions, and it creates an image. Lewis also said, "To combine these elements, the positioning statement should be designed to create an image reflecting the perception of the hotel that management wishes its target market to hold and reflecting promises on which the brand can deliver and make good."[4] The subtext of this definition is that the key to a hotel's position lies in how it is viewed by the customer.

Through market research, hoteliers can determine which attributes travelers (or travel managers) consider in choosing a hotel brand and how travelers view a brand in light of those attributes. Using that information, the researcher can apply discriminant analysis to develop a "map" of the brand's position as seen by its customers.[5] In assessing those attributes, researchers must be careful to distinguish the *determinant* attributes (those that actually cause a purchase) from *salient* attributes (those that are top-of-mind but may not actually distinguish the hotel). In terms of positioning, the distinction between determinant and salient attributes might not be so keenly noticed, because both contribute to the view that a customer has of a given brand's position. It is possible, however, to establish positioning maps based solely on determinant attributes.[6]

BUSINESS TRAVELERS

The attributes travelers use to determine their view of a hotel brand's position vary by traveler class. Moreover, even travelers who use the same attributes assign varying weights to those attributes. A principal point of differentiation among travelers is whether they are traveling on business or for pleasure. This study examined hotel brands' positions among business travelers only. As a proxy for the travelers themselves, data were collected from corporate travel managers and travel agents whose clients were chiefly business travelers. At the time of the study some observers estimated that such channels delivered 25 percent of all hotel room reservations. That percentage is higher for upscale hotels than for midmarket and economy properties.

The Study

SAMPLES AND DATA

Data for the study described in this chapter were drawn from summary statistics published in the yearly U.S. Hotel Systems Survey for 1989, 1990, and 1991 by *Business Travel News*.[7] The survey compiles the views of corporate travel managers and business travel agents' opinions of the nation's hotel brands on a variety of attributes.

At the time the data were compiled the hotel industry was at the bottom of its worst shakeout in at least two decades. In 1991 the U.S. hotel industry's average occupancy dropped to 60.8 percent, a twenty-year low.[8] Moreover, many hotels were in the red. A study revealed that in 1990 U.S. hotels lost some $5.5 billion and another $2.7 billion in 1991.[9] Coopers and Lybrand estimated that

60 percent of hotels were operating at a loss in mid-1992. Data from Smith Travel Research suggested that increases in hotels' average daily room rate (ADR) lagged the consumer price index from 1987 to 1991.[10] The supply of new hotel rooms was vastly outstripping demand. This period was chosen for the study because of the challenging hotel industry environment, which would likely cause many positioning changes.

Hotel brands were divided a priori by *Business Travel News* into five market segments: luxury, upscale, midprice, economy, and all-suite. Because of the number of hotel brands under consideration, each respondent rated hotel chains in only one or two segments. The attributes used to create perceptual maps for the upscale segment (the segment chosen to illustrate the mapping technique), in order of importance, were quality of food; physical appearance/in-room amenities; helpful, courteous staff; facilities for nonresort meetings; overall price-value; overall average rating, facilities for resort meetings; ease of arranging individual travel; ease in arranging group travel; timely commission payments; frequent-traveler programs; and corporate discount programs.

The survey's sampling method remained consistent over the three-year period, each year involving approximately seventy-five hundred randomly selected subscribers who were business travel managers or travel agents focusing on business accounts. Because the samples do not meet statistical standards required to rule out sampling bias or errors, any projections to the industry at large should be made with caution. Nevertheless, the data provided a positioning map of several chains based on travel manager and agent perceptions.[11]

Respondents rating each hotel brand were asked whether they had booked their clients into a property affiliated with a given hotel brand in the previous twelve months. A respondent's attribute ratings for that brand were tabulated only if the respondent answered this question in the affirmative. The consequence of this methodology is that the sample size from brand to brand in the same year's survey shows considerable variation.

ANALYSIS

The goal was to create perceptual maps showing the relative positions of the various brands and to examine movements in a brand's position over the three years. Analyses of the relative positions of the ten most-used brands in each tier in the data published in 1990 were conducted and the results were compared with those brands' positions in 1991 and 1992. Each analysis was conducted for thirty hotel brands (ten brands for each of three years in each market segment). Also, the positions of the top two brands in each of the five tiers over the three years were analyzed (another thirty-brand analysis).

The outcome of the analysis was perceptual maps revealing how each brand was positioned relative to its competitors and how each brand's position changed over the three years studied. The goal was to test statistically the changes in market position over time to determine the extent to which brands occupy the same perceptual space from one year to the next.

The process entailed probabilistic multidimensional scaling (MDS) algorithms to derive the coordinates for the perceptual map.[12] Multidimensional scaling is a method that can be used for calculating similarities among objects by a set of attributes. The calculations result in coordinates that can be plotted using coordinate axes to form a map. The distances thus calculated indicate the extent to which the respondents view brands as similar.

Positions of the brands on the map can assist managers in identifying potential competitive threats and opportunities. The coordinates of a brand's location on the X and Y axes reflect underlying composites of attitudes toward the brands among the survey respondents, with each quadrant representing values along one axis that measures marketing programs and the other that measures product/service quality. It is important to bear in mind that the "distances" are in psychological space, measured in terms of customer perceptions and preferences.[13]

It is also important to note that perceptual maps are essentially value neutral: no spot on the map is inherently better or worse than another is, unless a chain intends to occupy a certain position (competitive set) and finds itself at another. Perceptual maps can indicate how "close" one's brand is to competing brands. Brands that are positioned relatively far from each other on the map are interpreted as less directly competitive, while hotel chains that have nearby coordinates are considered strongly competitive. The map can also identify open space, which is interpreted as an available market niche either for repositioning existing operations or for a new entrant.

Because it was possible to test for the significance of differences between points on the perceptual map, it was also possible to determine which chains occupied positions that were at significant distances apart. It was also possible to tell whether a movement by a brand from year to year was significant. Probabilistic scaling made it possible to focus only on statistically significant position differences. Such an approach clears much of the clutter surrounding position differences.

The outcome of the calculations was a set of points on a map. The location of each hotel brand was depicted according to how customers perceived them on the abovementioned attribute dimensions. Although the brands were arrayed on coordinate axes, their positions relative to the axes (and attributes) were less important than their positions relative to one another or changes in a brand's own position from one year to another were. Statistically significant changes in perceptual distances experienced by a brand over time were labeled "direction," while changes that involved motions that were not statistically significant were labeled "drift."

CARTOGRAPHY

Statistical tests were used to examine whether the points on the coordinate axes were at significant distances from each other. The maps were constructed so as to allow them to be overlaid. Differences shown in two dimensions may be greater in three dimensions. Circles drawn around the points on a map depicted clusters of points that are not at statistically significant distances from each other.

MAPPING CHANGES

After the 1990 map was constructed, each successive map (for 1991 and 1992) allowed two levels of analysis. It was possible to compare the chains' relative positions against each other as well as to compare the positions of each chain in 1991 with its 1990 position (and the positions of each in 1992 with its 1991 position). Indeed, there was considerable movement in managers' and agents' perceptions of the chains' positions.

The data published in 1992 recorded the positions held by hotel brands in the nightmare year of 1991, when it appeared that the industry would never recover from the effects of war, overbuilding, and recession. Ironically, the competitive clusters found in the 1992 data were similar to those in the baseline 1990 chart.

BRAND MOVEMENT

The perceptual maps indicated how individual brands did or did not attempt to change customers' perceptions of their positions. The maps captured the movements of individual brands from year to year based on customers' perceptions of differences in attributes among the chains. The decisions brands made to emphasize one or another discriminating dimension shifted their position in the minds of their customers.

To illustrate how the maps indicate relative positioning, consider that, on the 1990 map, Stouffer was on par with Inter-Continental on price and product quality, in the upper-right quadrant. That is, their points on the map were close enough to put them in the same competitive set. In 1991, however, customers' price-value perception of Stouffer moved it away from Inter-Continental's competitive set (as both moved to the lower-right quadrant but farther apart), a movement that was reversed in 1992 following considerable advertising, acquisitions, and product upgrades (with both moving high up the vertical axis, Stouffer into the upper-left quadrant and Inter-Continental into the upper-right).

To take another example, Marriott moved downward on the cost scale between 1990 and 1991 (within the lower-right quadrant). The chain responded to the hotel industry's recession (and its own real estate–driven difficulties) by emphasizing the economic dimension—particularly its incentive programs. For example, Marriott beefed up its frequent-guest and corporate-discount programs and courted travel agents and managers by guaranteeing commission payments in thirty days. By 1992 that focus was softened and the chain moved up but far to the left, where it found itself competing with Hyatt and less with Hilton and Sheraton, as it had the previous year.

Actionable Insights

Managers should monitor the implications of their marketing strategies. They need to examine the attributes that customers use to differentiate one hotel brand from another, checking the dimensions on which that position is based for both their own brand and competing brands. Ratings such as those compiled by *Business Travel News* can indicate to marketing managers the effectiveness over time of their brands' marketing strategies in positioning against the competition.

Such an approach could help hoteliers avoid making the mistake of presuming a competitive set based only on physical attributes. Two similar-appearing brands may or may not actually compete directly against each other, and not all upscale brands are part of a given competitive set. By developing a perceptual map, a brand's manager could determine which brands are actually in the brand's competitive set. More important, by maintaining such a perceptual map over time, a manager could assess whether changes in the brand's marketing strategy were causing the hotel's position to change. Changes in position should be intentional and not accidental. Otherwise, a brand can find itself competing in a set that puts it at a disadvantage.

On the other hand, intentional changes in the competitive set can make sense. Marriott's forty-nine-dollar-room program, for instance, substantially changed its position on the 1991 map, compared with those of 1990 and 1992. For that time, the brand moved out of one competitive set and into another one. The data set does not indicate intention, but it may be inferred that Marriott's move was a deliberate strategy. While the technique in this example is based on historical data, the lessons pertaining to how a hotel's position moves as a result of marketing changes—intentional or unintentional—can be used for future strategic planning.

In 1992, for example, Ramada launched an advertising campaign with the following positioning statement: "Ramada's in, Holiday's out." Ramada's president Stephen Belmonte explained the strategy as one of positioning Ramada close to Holiday Inn in the customer's mind or, in other words, to position Ramada with Holiday Inn in the customer's consideration set.[14] The strategy was chosen, Belmonte said, because Ramada was "a sleepy and stagnant company" with an "identity crisis" and was falling out of favor as a midmarket brand.[15] According to Scott Deaver, Ramada's vice president of marketing, the objective of the campaign was for "Ramada to be part of a 'competitive pair' with Holiday Inn in the same way that Reebok and Nike, Burger King and McDonald's, or MCI and AT&T are competitive pairs." In commenting on the results of the campaign, Deaver noted that there was no way of knowing whether the campaign achieved its objective of having Ramada considered with Holiday Inn.[16] This chapter has shown that it is quite possible to know such a thing by using perceptual maps.

---

1 Robert C. Lewis, "Advertising Your Hotel's Position," *Cornell Hotel and Restaurant Administration Quarterly* 31, no. 2 (1990): 85.

2 Mark Harris, "Economical Positioning," *Cornell Hotel and Restaurant Administration Quarterly* 29, no. 2 (1988): 97.

3 Lewis, "Advertising Your Hotel's Position," 87.

4 Robert C. Lewis, "The Positioning Statement for Hotels," *Cornell Hotel and Restaurant Administration Quarterly* 22, no. 1 (1981): 53.

5 For an explanation of discriminant analysis, see Robert C. Lewis, "The Market Position: Mapping Guests' Perceptions of Hotel Operations," *Cornell Hotel and Restaurant Administration Quarterly* 26, no. 2 (1985): 88–89.

6 Lewis, "The Market Position," 93.

7 *Business Travel News,* January 29, 1990, 36–41; January 28, 1991, 13–19; and January 27, 1992, 15–18.

8 Pauline Yoshihashi, "Hotel Recovery Will Be a Late Arrival," *Wall Street Journal,* July 27, 1992, B1.

9 Ibid.

10 Ibid.

11 The data used for this study were selected to illustrate the perceptual-mapping method and should not be used for strategic interpretation of the upscale lodging market.

12 J. O. Ramsay, "Some Statistical Approaches to Multidimensional Scaling," *Journal of the Royal Statistical Society,* ser. A, 145, no. 3 (1982): 285–312; and Mark L. Davison, *Multidimensional Scaling* (New York: John Wiley and Sons, 1983).

13 The significance of psychological positioning is explored in George Overstreet, "Creating Value in Oversupplied Markets: The Case of Charlottesville, Virginia, Hotels," *Cornell Hotel and Restaurant Administration Quarterly* 34, no. 5 (1993): 84–91.

14 David A. Aaker and J. Gary Shansby, "Positioning Your Product," *Business Horizons* 5, no. 3 (1982): 56–62; see also Michael S. Morgan, "Traveler's Choice: The Effects of Advertising and Prior Stay," *Cornell Hotel and Restaurant Administration Quarterly* 32, no. 4 (1991): 40–49.

15 Philip Swan, "Raging Belmonte," *Lodging* 70, no. 10 (1992): 28–29.

16 Jim Galb, "Taking off the Gloves," *ASTA Agency Management* 66, no. 8 (1993): 95.

CHAPTER NINE

Brand Extensions and Customer Loyalty

Building and successfully managing strong brands is considered a key driver of success in the hotel industry. CEOs of hotel companies that own brands recognize that brand equity drives stock price and shareholder value. Consumers often base their hotel stay decisions on their perception of a specific hotel's brand name. The United States now has well over three hundred hotel brands competing for business, more than in any other product category. Many of these brands are extensions of existing brand names.

The Challenge

Brand extension is the practice of introducing a new brand (differentiated by market segment) using a well-established brand name as leverage. Most major hotel companies have at least one brand extension, implying that hotel chains consider the strategy to be successful. There are two dangers in creating multiple extensions, however. First, managing many brands can complicate and possibly overwhelm the core corporate structure. Second, having the same name on a large number of products can wear out the parent brand's equity. That second possibility is the topic of the study presented in this chapter. Before considering a brand extension, a hotel firm must evaluate the potential influence on the brand as a whole. This study attempted to estimate empirically whether brand extensions encourage guests to repeat their stay with a particular chain's brands.

A brand extension strategy allows firms to penetrate a variety of market segments with differentiated products that carry a single, well-established brand name. Hotel firms see several advantages to brand extensions, including quicker acceptance of new products by consumers, economies of scale in marketing-support expenditures, lower risk associated with introduction of new products, and guest retention.[1] In using brand extensions, however, there are also disadvantages, including managerial complexities (corporate structure needed to support multiple brands and monitoring the performance of multiple operational units), marketing issues (positioning the brand and achieving clarity in the associated marketing message and avoiding brand cannibalization), and challenges in customer relationship management (establishing and maintaining brand-specific customer service quality standards).[2]

The research presented here sought to provide insights into the brand extension phenomenon in the lodging industry by testing whether hotels can increase customer loyalty by introducing brand extensions. This study posited that brand extensions can increase customer loyalty by increasing the switching costs from a particular brand family to a competitor's brand. With extensions, firms can reach distinguishable groups of consumers with diverse needs. Customers familiar with a brand are more likely to patronize an extension of that brand than they are to take risks with an unfamiliar brand (a risk that is part of switching costs). If there is an "extension effect," the probability of a customer's staying within a corporate brand family (or, equivalently, a brand system or a brand portfolio) will be proportionally greater than the number of brands offered by that corporation, all other factors being equal.[3] This chapter presents the findings of the study and discusses their relevance to and potential applications in the lodging industry.

The Study

CORPORATE EXTENSION

The literature on brand extensions suggests that hotels can use brand extensions to influence consumer brand choices. Since product differentiation allows markets to be segmented by product variety, less intervariety competition takes place as differentiation increases.[4] Thus, for example, the old one-size-fits-all, full-service hotel finds itself losing customers at the margin as they seek carefully targeted products. The result of increased differentiation is that new entrants may be deterred by the barrier of learning costs.[5] Brand extensions are believed to be an appropriate approach to breaking the entry barriers between product categories through the carryover of a brand's reputation.[6]

Corporate extension occurs when a corporate brand is the endorsing brand (or master brand) that launches sub-brands (or differentiated brands) into various product-quality levels.[7] Examples of such extension include DKNY by Donna Karan, Chaps by Ralph Lauren, Holiday Inn Express by Holiday Inn, and Courtyard by Marriott. Based on the variables defined above, an "extension and brand switching" (EABS) model was developed to estimate customer-retention rates for a firm with brand extensions.

The study also examined the extension effect by market segment. There is some support in the literature for treating business and leisure travelers differently because customers in these two segments have distinct needs and respond differently to marketing stimuli. Therefore, the study analyzed the relationship between extension and brand switching for both the business and leisure segments.

The literature on brand switching has shown that many other factors in addition to brand extension affect brand switching.[8] While control variables were not addressed explicitly in this study, they were included in the analysis. Based on a review of the relevant literature, the following control variables that could potentially influence a customer's choice among alternative brands were identified: brand availability, switching cost, extension, price, preference, and search costs.

Measuring Brand Names

The study measured the main effect of the brand extension variable by the number of brand names in the product line. As the number of brands within a family rises, the probability of switching to brands outside the family should decrease. That effect can be attributed to the dominance of the parent brand caused by the synergy of promoting a common name across a number of market segments. Alternatively, however, extension could dilute the brand; that is, as the number of extensions increases, switching out of the brand would also increase. If that were true, there would be a nonlinear effect of the number of brand extensions on brand switching. The study therefore investigated empirically whether brand switching has a straight-line relationship with extensions or one that is U shaped.

Several controls were estimated for this part of the study, although they are not discussed in this chapter. Availability is the number of properties a brand has in various markets. Switching costs were measured by frequency of hotel stays prior to the current stay, advertising was measured by a brand's advertising expenditures, and publicity was measured by a public ranking of hotel chains. Price was measured using the actual prices of the hotel at the current stay and next stay, along with price dispersion across brands reflected in the number of prices facing a consumer and the variability among those prices.

Preference was used to measure changes in travel destination, changes in location, changes from a suite to a nonsuite hotel, changes from a resort to a non-resort hotel, and changes to a different price tier. Market search was measured using time between visits, a prior stay's level of satisfaction, number of nights stayed per hotel visit, group size, whether the customer had visited the hotel before, and whether the customer traveled outside the immediate geographical region. Demographic characteristics included income, employment status, educational attainment, and travel intensity during the preceding twelve months.

Data and Variables

The lodging industry was chosen for this study because it employs brand extensions on a widespread basis, providing a rich context within which to test the hypotheses. By one estimate, nearly 70 percent of all hotels in the United States are branded.[9] Most of these are small chains, although some chains are large indeed. While the number of chains is smaller in Europe and Asia than it is in the United States, that number is growing rapidly. Brand managers and franchisees alike would benefit from knowing whether extensions are associated with customer loyalty, a source of significant revenue and profit for both.

The data for the study were drawn from two sources. The first part comprises consumer-survey data collected by D. K. Shifflet and Associates, including only respondents who made at least two hotel stays in consecutive months during the most recent three-month period. These survey data included information on individual prices paid, trip context, and customer characteristics.

The second data set consisted of lodging-firm characteristics collected from secondary sources: parent-company affiliation, member brands, advertising expenditures, and numbers of units. This secondary data covered 88 brands. Of those 88 brands, 42 had no extension, 16 had one extension, 13 had two extensions, 12 had three extensions, and 5 had four extensions. The secondary data corresponded to a time period that was comparable to that of the survey data.

Two additional variables were generated after the data were merged. The length of corporate extensions was calculated as the number of line brand names a corporation has in the survey data set. The number of lodging firms in a metropolitan statistical area (MSA) was calculated from the survey data according to the parent brand information collected.

Only observations for the most recent two hotel stays for each respondent were retained, leaving a data set comprising 31,467 observations. Using only the most recent stays minimizes recall bias as much as possible.[10] Standard techniques were applied to handle the missing observations.[11] For efficiency, a random sub-sample of 6,840 observations was used for final analysis; among these about 80 percent, or 5,414 observations, were used for model calibration and the remaining 20 percent, or 1,426 observations, were used as a holdout sample for testing the model's predictive ability. The analysis data set included information for forty-six parent hotel brands, representing all the large hotel chains operating in the United States.

To account for the effect of price, three control variables were used: reference price, current price, and market concentration.[12] Reference price is the price paid during the first stay, while current price is the price paid during the second stay. Market concentration is the number of brands in the market during the second stay. To account for changes in context, change in destination, change in location, familiarity with the destination from a prior stay, and satisfaction with first stay's brand family were included as factors. Income (on a twenty-category scale) and occupation (professional or not) were used to account for consumer characteristics.

Overall, 65 percent of the travelers in our sample switched brands from the first stay to the second. This is a measure of customer turnover (not to be confused with sales turnover, which is used as a measure of sales in some countries). Any action that managers can take to reduce customer turnover could result in higher financial performance by lowering customer-acquisition costs. Almost all the measures described above proved reliable according to statistical tests.

Results

The question at issue in the study was whether brand extensions can help lower customer turnover level. The study was the first empirical attempt to derive the ideal number of extensions beyond which switching is likely. This was its main and most significant contribution to the literature on brand management.

THREE'S A CHARM

Customers are less likely to switch brands when the length of brand extension is around three.[13] That is, when they offer up to three extensions, brands are able to retain additional customers by offering a choice of segments under the same name. Apparently, by the time a brand has three extensions it has attained a critical mass in terms of customer awareness and recognition. Furthermore, offering three extensions balances the choices offered to customers against the extent to which a concept can realistically be stretched before the brand extension begins to undermine the customer's belief that one brand name can, in fact, offer a meaningful choice in widely diverse segments.

Below three extensions, the switching rate rises, perhaps because the number of choices is too limited to cover a wide enough set of customer needs. With one or two extensions, the resources used to promote the brand are often limited. Moreover, consumers would rather stay with the one brand that satisfies their needs, in the absence of intervening factors, than find an almost-right brand. With the increasing popularity of frequent-user programs that reward and recognize users of a brand family, this effect is likely to be magnified. To frame the discussion in another way, typical consumers often consider hotel brands for three types of purchase occasions: business trips, conference attendance, and vacations. If travelers could patronize one brand with three extensions that met their needs for each of those three travel purposes (and could collect rewards to boot), they might be prompted to keep all their business with one hotel brand family.

Beyond three extensions, however, the switching rate rises. As the results of the study suggest, stretching a brand beyond three extensions (that is, into several diverse market segments), may strain customers' credulity. There comes a point at which customers tend to lower their patronage of a brand if it tries to cover too many distinct market segments, overly diluting its brand position. Another possible reason for this nonlinear effect is that too many extensions may dilute the company's support of each individual brand, not to mention confusing or alienating consumers.

The analysis revealed no significant differences between the business and leisure segments in terms of the three-brand extension length. This means that, when it comes to maintaining loyalty, business and leisure travelers respond similarly to brand extensions. That is, the brand extension effect is a customer-level phenomenon that does not vary by trip purpose.

Thus, contrary to other findings, this study strongly suggests not only that there is an optimum number of hotel brands within a family but also that this number appears to be three.[14] Beyond three extensions, lodging firms are overextending their brands, with potentially unsatisfactory outcomes. Brand switching decreases as a brand family grows to about three extensions, but rises with further extensions.

Cautious Interpretation

This study was not expected to be the final word on this topic, and the results should be interpreted with caution. First, because the data are correlational, reverse causation is possible, wherein low switching rates may cause firms to create brand extensions. The original findings are, however, based on robust tests of association between extension and loyalty. Second, only the direct or main effects were tested; no interactions among the control variables were estimated. These cautions notwithstanding, the results validate expectations based on a sound theoretical model and thus provide a high level of confidence in the applicability of the theory.

Hotels can favorably influence consumer choice through marketing activities that emphasize multiple brand extensions. Effective brand extensions seem likely to increase customer loyalty and promote repeat buying. The risk of disappointment with an unknown brand deters consumers from switching from a more familiar brand to a less familiar one. Put another way, customers who perceive that a particular brand's mainline hotel offers high quality will be more likely to patronize that brand's specialized-market hotels (and vice versa). Extending the analysis, if consumers tend toward brand loyalty to avoid switching costs, hotel firms can exercise price discrimination and charge higher prices to their loyal customers.

It appears that corporate extensions in the lodging industry might be most helpful in retaining customers when extensions involve about three hotel tiers. For brands that have no extensions, this finding suggests that opportunities exist for appropriate corporate extension in reasonable numbers of brands and in diverse geographical locations. Even venerable hotel brands such as Four Seasons and Ritz-Carlton, which once had no brand extensions, are offering customers multiple options (hotels, resorts, residences) for a variety of purchase occasions.

A Framework for Decisions

This research is perhaps the first attempt to relate consumer-purchase data with brand use and extension and to learn about the effects of brand extensions on consumers' buying behavior. The study offers a valuable conceptual and analytical framework for brand management. Consider the following two examples from a wide range of research applications.

Industry Level. Regarding industry fundamentals, analysts have been interested in the degree of brand switching from high-price brands or brand extensions to low-price brands or brand extensions during periods of economic slowdown, as well as in the degree of subsequent shifts upward during periods of economic prosperity. The issue has implications, for example, for the relative stability or volatility of earnings for lodging companies concentrated in one or two price segments compared with companies with brands or brand extensions across the price spectrum. Longitudinal data spanning business cycles would help us understand this phenomenon better.

Company Level. From a company perspective, the utility of analyzing customers' switching behavior among brands is not limited to a company's own brand family but is valuable for a more comprehensive understanding of the demand curves that each of its brands faces, knowledge plainly applicable to better revenue management. Loyal customers are price insensitive compared with brand-shifting patrons, and loyal customers may not need as substantial a price promotion to encourage purchase as would a first-time customer. Degrees of customers' brand loyalty can be factored into the next generation of revenue management systems to help determine the extent of rate adjustments.

While brand extension is a promising avenue for management action and further exploration, it is not without peril. As this study demonstrated, brand managers can go too far in extending their brands. Too great an extension may invite negative consequences for the entire brand family by raising the rate at which customers defect from the brand. Navigating the fine line between underuse of an important asset and its overextension is where the opportunity to maximize a brand's value lies. The results of this study should provide brand managers with added insight into the potentials and perils of brand extension.

---

1 For marketing-support expenditures, see David Arnold, *The Handbook of Brand Management* (Reading, MA: Addison-Wesley, 1992), 142; for introduction of new products, see Jean-Noel Kapferer, *Strategic Brand Management* (New York: Free Press, 1992), 113.

2 See David A. Aaker and Kevin L. Keller, "Consumer Evaluations of Brand Extensions," *Journal of Marketing* 54, no. 1 (1990): 27–41; Peter H. Farquhar, Julia A. Han, Paul M. Herr, and Yuji Ijiri, "Strategies for Leveraging Master Brands: How to Bypass the Risks of Direct Extensions," *Marketing Research* 4, no. 3 (1992): 32–43; Barbara Loken and Deborah R. John, "Diluting Brand Beliefs: When Do

Brand Extensions Have a Negative Impact?" *Journal of Marketing* 57, no. 3 (1993): 71–84; David A. Aaker, *Building Strong Brands* (New York: Free Press, 1996), 240; and Byung-Do Kim and Mary W. Sullivan, "The Effect of Parent Brand Experience on Line Extension Trial and Repeat Purchase," *Marketing Letters* 9, no. 2 (1998): 181–93.

3 First, it is assumed that customers have at least some information about whether a brand is an extension of a given corporation. Otherwise, the extension is meaningless. Second, the meaning of a "proportional" draw is as follows: Suppose a market has two corporations, where one has two brands and the other has three, assuming all brands are equivalent. If there is no extension influence, the first corporation will draw a two-fifths portion of customers and the other three-fifths, other factors remaining equal. If there is a positive effect of the extension length (the number of sub-brands) of the second corporation, it will draw more than three-fifths of the total customers. If the extension effect is negative, the second corporation will draw less than three-fifths of the total customers.

4 Norman J. Ireland, *Product Differentiation and Quality: The New Industrial Economics,* ed. G. Norman and M. La Manna (Brookfield, VT: Edward Elgar, 1993), 84.

5 Jean Gabszewicz, Lynne Pepall, and Jacques-Francois Thisse, "Sequential Entry with Brand Loyalty Caused by Consumer Learning-by-Using," *Journal of Industrial Economics* 40, no. 4 (1992): 397–416.

6 See Bruce Lyons, "Barriers to Entry," in *Economics of Industrial Organization: Surveys in Economics,* ed. Stephen Davies and Bruce Lyons with Huw Dixon and Paul Geroski (New York: Longman Group UK, 1988), 45–46; Arnold, *The Handbook of Brand Management,* 142; C. J. Choi and Carlo Scarpa, "Credible Spatial Preemption through Reputation Extension," *International Journal of Industrial Organization* 10, no. 3 (1992): 439–47; Henry G. Grabowski and John M. Vernon, "Brand Loyalty, Entry, and Price Competition in Pharmaceuticals after the 1984 Drug Act," *Journal of Law and Economics* 35, no. 2 (1992): 331–50; Richard J. Gilbert and Carmen Matutes, "Product-Line Rivalry with Brand Differentiation," *Journal of Industrial Economics* 41, no. 3 (1993): 223–40; and Aaker, *Building Strong Brands,* 277, 295.

7 Farquhar, Peter H., Julia A. Han, Paul M. Herr, and Yuji Ijiri, "Strategies for Leveraging Master Brands: How to Bypass the Risks of Direct Extensions," *Marketing Research* 4, no. 3 (1992): 32–43.

8 Michael S. Morgan and Chekitan S. Dev, "An Empirical Study of Brand Switching for a Retail Service," *Journal of Retailing* 70, no. 3 (1994): 267–82.

9 Stephen Rushmore, "Hotel Franchising: How to Be a Successful Franchisee," *Real Estate Journal,* Summer 1997, 56.

10 Morgan and Dev, "An Empirical Study of Brand Switching."

11 Missing values of a categorical variable were put into a separate category. In the process, it was assumed that the observations were homogeneous in that category. The effect of that category was not interpreted. Missing values of a continuous variable were replaced with the means that were calculated based on the observations with profiles similar to those of missing observations.

12 See Russell S. Winer, "A Reference Price Model of Brand Choice for Frequently Purchased Products," *Journal of Consumer Research* 13, no. 2 (1986): 250–56.

13 This number was obtained by direct calculation of the estimated equation (1) for values of the number of extensions ranging from 0 to 6. Usual calculus methods were not used (and not appropriate), because this variable takes only integers as values.

14 For contrary findings, see Jean-Noel Kapferer, *Strategic Brand Management* (New York: Free Press, 1992), 188–89; and Aaker, *Building Strong Brands,* 243, 264.

Taj Hotels, Resorts, and Palaces

The case study presented in this chapter offers a framework for innovation, the *7-I process,* and examines the factors that underlie successful service innovations within the framework of a comprehensive and integrated innovation-management model.

The Challenge

They say that an excellent hotel generates few complaints.[1] Yet hearing few complaints may mean that honest guest feedback is not being heard, not that guests are satisfied. An inefficient or inaccurate system for registering and responding to guest complaints breeds poor performance. Since handling complaints is an integral part of any service operation, it is important to develop an effective complaint-management system. Moreover, hotel employees often fail to share complaints, fearing that management will think poorly of them. This chapter describes an innovative complaint-management system that was implemented at the Taj Holiday Village Goa during an upgrade of the hotel's entire operation. The system has the potential to enable hotel operators to register complaints accurately and respond to them effectively without discouraging employees from reporting them.

At the Taj Goa, complaint resolution was a key impediment to meeting management objectives. The novel complaint resolution method described here formed the basis of the improvements that allowed the Taj Goa to upgrade its operation from three to five stars. The hotel's management applied a seven-step innovation model, the abovementioned 7-I model.

The Setting

The Taj Holiday Village Goa is a 142-room, five-star property operated by the Indian-based Taj Hotels, Resorts, and Palaces. Taj opened the Holiday Village resort in 1982, operating it as a three-star property. The main clientele is leisure, with approximately 15 to 20 percent conference business. The guests include mainly Indians, Western Europeans, Americans, and East Asians. Guests provide feedback through the hotel's Guest Satisfaction Tracking System.

The Taj Goa's management team wanted to reposition it as a five-star resort and make it a market leader in Goa, whereupon it renovated the property completely to match international standards. It also wanted to redefine the hotel's "servicescape" to match its new image. To this end, extensive training sessions and certification tests were conducted to develop the necessary skills and attitudes among employees. In spite of these efforts, however, the hotel had yet to occupy its true market position after the first year following renovation. The RevPAR index remained at 0.96, barely at par with the market, and the "top box" guest satisfaction scores (guest giving the hotel the highest rating) remained only a little above 30 percent.[2] At this point, the hotel embraced the 7-I approach to innovation.

The 7-I Approach to Hospitality Innovation

The seven steps involved in the 7-I process are *inspiration, insight, ideation, initiative, implementation, invigilation,* and *investigation.* Every step depends in part on the preceding step as the innovation is gradually modified and refined until it achieves the goal.

INSPIRATION

Inspiration initiates and guides the change process. It involves conscious discovery of the reality of a situation and then drives the strategy to alter that reality. At the Taj Goa, hotel employees were made aware of the new objective—to become a five-star resort for the leisure and tourist market—a lofty objective that instilled pride in employees and management alike. Everyone knew that working for a five-star property would mean providing the highest-quality professional service and amenities to the hotel's guests.

Employees are inspired when management is open and transparent about its objectives, sharing the true status of the company, because it makes them feel valued and trusted. At the Taj Goa the general manager informed all employees that the hotel was lagging behind its competition in terms of ADR (average daily room rate), RevPAR, and occupancy.[3] The general manager's outreach combined with the ambitious nature of the target outcome inspired the team to undertake the innovation process wholeheartedly.

Insight

Insight helps turn inspiration into results because innovation requires deep understanding of the processes that are to undergo change. Every step toward understanding relevant environmental factors needs a moment of insight. In a hospitality environment, in which it is not possible to run controlled experiments to test the elements of the change process, insight plays a critical role.

At the Taj Goa, personalizing the guest experience was the critical factor, and it found insights in the Four Seasons model.[4] The personalized service Four Seasons provides keeps it on top of the market.[5] The Taj Goa sought insights into how to personalize its service to meet its guests' high expectations. The concept of personalizing service provided a framework within which to absorb insightful knowledge that can be applied in developing definitive guest experiences, generating higher guest satisfaction, and increasing revenue.[6]

To redesign its services, the Taj Goa sought guest feedback on its existing operations through its proprietary customer feedback system, through which employees upload guest feedback that is available on a real-time basis to top hotel as well as corporate management.

This process revealed another insight into the guest feedback process: not all feedback channels are equally attractive to guests. Research shows, for example, that guests are disinclined to use guest room comment cards. Direct conversations with hotel management are more likely to yield useful information, as 49 percent of guests prefer registering complaints with a manager rather than with a frontline employee or on an in-room comment card.[7]

Ideation

It is through ideation that a change management team develops new ideas directed at solving problems.[8] An innovative idea must be grounded in reality and bear directly on key factors in the change process. All stakeholders—employees, management, and guests—should become part of the idea-generating process, because an idea that is not supported by all stakeholders is unlikely to take hold. Full stakeholder buy-in facilitates effective implementation of an idea. Transparency and full participation lead to a richer understanding of the ideation process and a better outcome.

The key idea in the Taj Goa's innovation plan was bypassing the cumbersome process of registering complaints in writing. Instead, employees would share guest complaints by telephoning a centralized guest services desk. When an employee receiving a guest complaint phoned guest services, the attendant would text a group short service message (GSSM) to the mobile phones of all heads of department and managers—instantly alerting every department about the complaint.

This innovative approach made computer access unnecessary, and most guest-facing employees carry mobile phones at all times. Once a complaint was texted, the responsible department could contact the guest and initiate service recovery. Other departments could also follow up by treating the guest with extra care, ensuring that the service lapse would not be repeated while enhancing the guest experience to compensate for the problem.

INITIATIVE

Even with inspiration and insight, a great idea can work effectively only if it is supported by an initiative, a plan of action through which an innovation is implemented. An effective initiative works as a catalyst between an idea and the implementation stage of the innovation cycle. The initiative stage is in that respect similar to the soft launch of a hotel. During such a trial period, employees and management can assess an idea's efficacy and identify opportunities for improvement. The initiative stage ensures that the idea is ready to be implemented and will remain on course following implementation.

When the Taj Goa's complaint management system was soft launched, the general manager observed that many complaints were "lost" in the course of daily operations. The team then sought to modify the system slightly to incorporate a complaint-tracking system in which every complaint would be recorded on a shared Excel spreadsheet. This system ensured that all complaints would be available to everyone with access to a computer. The general manager would review each day's complaints to monitor service recovery, ensuring that the hotel's senior management team learned of and could effectively track guest complaints and that most guests leaving the hotel would depart happy.

Yet the new system for sharing complaints made managers who were responsible for departments in which complaints occurred uncomfortable, because employees could now communicate a complaint directly to guest services without first checking with their own department managers. This led most managers and department heads to discourage their employees from communicating complaints. This caused the general manager once again to change the process so that an employee reporting a complaint would inform the appropriate departmental manager after reporting it. Employees were assured that they would not be disciplined for reporting complaints. Department heads were also told that the process was being run on a test case basis and that it would not affect their performance appraisals. Since complaints from any department reflect poorly on the department manager, it took some time for the entire team to commit to sharing guest complaints openly.

IMPLEMENTATION

The real test of an idea takes place during implementation, which depends on effective communication with all stakeholders. Rarely do those who develop an idea assume primary responsibility for its implementation. Implementation therefore reveals gaps in understanding between management and frontline employees. Moreover, during implementation the scale at which an idea is to be implemented typically broadens. An idea that tests well in a small focus group might fare worse when introduced across the property. Thus, the real-world test of an innovation process is crucial. It can require considerable agility and finesse on the part of management to navigate around glitches and misunderstandings. Buy-in can dissolve rapidly with major failures.

At the Taj Goa, the general manager announced the new role for guest services through the revamped complaint management system at one of the hotel's monthly staff meetings. He explained the rationale for the innovation and the process involved in operating the new system. He met with the employees' union separately to ensure that all union members understood what the process was designed to achieve. Those responsible for training departmental staff were trained in the operation of the process first, and these departmental trainers in turn trained the remaining staff.[9]

Ironically, the implementation of the complaint process created an awkward outcome, given its goal of reducing service lapses—a noticeable increase in complaints registered. This clearly demonstrated the system's success, but it also created a delicate situation because capturing all complaints made the Taj Goa's complaint rates seem high in comparison with those of other Taj hotels. Indeed, corporate management noticed the number of complaints and queried the general manager, who replied that higher awareness of guest complaints made it possible to address those complaints effectively—thereby eventually raising guest satisfaction scores.

Fortunately, that prediction was borne out when, once the system was fully in place, guest satisfaction rose almost 10 percent, RevPAR rose by one thousand rupees (about twenty dollars), and the RevPAR index rose to 1.10—a remarkable swing from below fair market share to 10 percent above it. Still, despite these favorable numbers, guest complaints increased at an even higher rate than did the guest satisfaction scores or the RevPAR index.

INVIGILATION

Once an innovation has been implemented, it must be invigilated, or monitored, to ensure that the process is running as intended. The long-term success of an innovation requires continual monitoring, supervision, and staff commitment—not to mention a good deal of hand-holding and a reliable training regime for new employees. Careful monitoring of the innovation process helps ensure full implementation, and observation based on invigilation can support modification as needed.

At the Taj Goa, invigilation led management to modify the complaint-monitoring plan, as guest dissatisfaction lingered even after complaints were reported and addressed. Despite an assertive service recovery process, guests rarely rated the hotel as "excellent" on guest satisfaction surveys. No matter how effectively a complaint was addressed, guests often recalled that something "not good" had occurred. Guest ratings of a hotel depend crucially on guest delight; the hotel can correct a problem but is forgiven only when the overall guest experience is highly positive.

Consequently the Taj Goa altered its program to include a proactive approach to determine guest preferences. Most upscale hotels send guests a pre-arrival questionnaire to learn about their personal preferences and to create a service blueprint. Research shows, however, that guests prefer face-to-face interaction with senior management.[10] Therefore the Taj Goa modified the guest complaint management system to include meetings between guests and senior managers. If a guest had a problem, a manager would be readily available to resolve the issue. While such personal contact might lead to yet another increase in the number of complaints, it would also ensure prompt service recovery and demonstrate to guests that their satisfaction was important.

Now every manager was responsible for meeting specified guests upon arrival to plan a customized experience. The manager would also be available for guests to call with suggestions, complaints, or inquiries. Once again, guest feedback was tracked on an Excel spreadsheet that would be updated following every guest encounter. This continual monitoring of the guest meeting process ensured that every guest would meet with a manager during a stay, helping the hotel understand and record individual guest needs, which in turn markedly improved the quality and quantity of information available to hotel staff.

Although frontline employees, who interacted most frequently with guests, were able to identify guest preferences, they had no incentive to share what they had learned. The general manager therefore created an incentive by rewarding employees for identifying a certain number of guest preferences each month. Staff also understood that delighted guests would leave higher tips, which led to increased reporting and recording of guest feedback.

INVESTIGATION

Proper invigilation makes it possible to investigate the various cause-and-effect relationships and unexpected outcomes that have occurred. Upon investigation it may be determined, for example, that seemingly unrelated services have affected an innovation's outcome. Investigation requires objective thinking and rigorous analysis. Analytical findings can then be used to fine-tune the servicescape.

At the Taj Village Goa, the guest-manager interaction process improved the quality of guest feedback dramatically. The ensuing investigation of guest dissatisfaction identified the following causes for 80 percent of the complaints:

- Room not ready on arrival
- Too long a wait for breakfast at the restaurant
- Inconsistent room servicing by housekeeping

Management analysis showed that unready rooms stemmed from hotel policy, which set both check-in and checkout at 12:00 p.m. All too often, departing guests did not leave until the noon deadline, leaving too little time for housekeeping to ready rooms for noon arrivals. The wait for breakfast occurred primarily because the restaurant provided too few covers for rooms and occupancy. This mismatch of restaurant size and guest patronage pressured the service staff and made guests wait longer. Finally, the housekeeping service inconsistency was caused by a combination of the check-in/checkout situation and ineffective training.

To solve the issue of unready rooms, the general manager requested corporate approval to shift the hotel's check-in time to 2:00 p.m. while keeping checkout time at noon. Adjusting the restaurant capacity was accomplished by shifting breakfast preparation work to a satellite kitchen to make room for more tables. With the check-in and checkout time resolved, management could focus on training to ensure housekeeping consistency. Whenever a housekeeper checked rooms, she would photograph mistakes, correct them, and take photographs to show the proper, corrected arrangement. Comparing the pictures at departmental briefings made it easy to clarify issues with room attendants and new incentive pay packages further motivated housekeeping staff to strive for excellence, as shown on guest satisfaction surveys.[11]

Results

The guest feedback innovation that was implemented at the Taj Goa helped reduce complaints dramatically and improve guest satisfaction scores by 20 percentage points on average. The hotel's RevPAR increased to the highest level in the market, with the RevPAR index moving up to 1.17, or 17 percent above its fair share of the market. In the process, the hotel became the market leader in Goa.

Based on an analysis of guest satisfaction scores from July 2006 to December 2008 and complaints for the corresponding periods, the correlation between the number of complaints and the corresponding overall satisfaction score for that month was statistically significant, demonstrating that the satisfaction scores had increased because of fewer complaints.[12] Increased interaction with guests and personalized service accounted for the remaining part of the increase in overall satisfaction.

Actionable Insights

This case study suggests that innovation in a hospitality operation is a complex process involving products, people, and processes. The use of the 7-I method at the Taj Goa took two years to show results—and then only after several midcourse adjustments. This required the identification and correction of a series of problems, some of which could not have been anticipated in the early stages of the process. By focusing on crucial organizational parameters, the Taj Goa was able to enjoy the fruits of a successful innovation.

---

1 Robert C. Lewis, "When Guests Complain," *Cornell Hotel and Restaurant Administration Quarterly* 24, no. 2 (1983): 23–32.

2 The RevPAR index is the revenue per available room of a particular hotel, divided by the average revenue per available room of the competitive set for that hotel.

3 Michael Ottenbacher and B. Gray, "The New Service Development Process: The Initial Stages for Hotel Innovations," *FIU Hospitality Review* 22, no. 2 (2004): 59–70.

4 Liana Victorino, Rohit Verma, Gerhard Plaschka, and Chekitan Dev, "Service Innovation and Customer Choices in the Hospitality Industry," *Managing Service Quality* 15, no. 6 (2005): 555–76.

5 Barbara Talbott, "The Power of Personal Service: Why it Matters; What Makes it Possible; How It Creates Competitive Advantage," *Cornell Hospitality Industry Perspectives* (Cornell Center for Hospitality Research), white paper no. 1 (2006), http://www.hotelschool.cornell.edu/chr/pdf/showpdf/chr/industry/powerpersonalservice.pdf?t=CHR&my_path_info=chr/industry/powerpersonalservice.pdf

6 Kesh Prasad and Chekitan Dev, "Model Estimates of Financial Impact of Guest Satisfaction Efforts," *Hotel and Motel Management* 217, no. 14 (2002): 23.

7 Alex M. Suskind, "An Examination of Guest Complaints and Complaint Communication Channels—the Medium Does Matter," *Cornell Hospitality Reports* (Cornell Center for Hospitality Research) 6, no. 14 (2006).

8 Peter Jones, "Managing Hospitality Innovation," *Cornell Hotel and Restaurant Administration Quarterly* 37, no. 5 (1996): 86.

9 Michael C. Ottenbacher, Vivienne Shaw, and M. Howley, "Impact of Employee Management on Hospitality Innovation Success," *FIU Hospitality and Tourism Review* 23, no. 1 (2005): 82–95.

10 Ibid.

11 Michael C. Sturman, "Using Your Pay System to Improve Employee Performance—How You Pay Makes a Difference," *Cornell Hospitality Reports* (Cornell Center for Hospitality Research) 6, no. 13 (2006).

12 SPSS 17.0 statistical computation software was used to determine these results.

▶ PART FOUR ◀

BRANDING EXECUTION

CHAPTER TEN

Managing Marketing and Branding Relationships

This chapter presents a study of marketing relationships between hotel brands and the properties with which they do business. In such relationships, both parties hope to minimize the costs of exchange. The chapter focuses on the development of governance mechanisms that can minimize those costs by preventing, or at least minimizing, the impact of *opportunism* on partners in a business relationship.

The Challenge

Opportunistic behavior, which includes dishonesty and neglecting obligations, is undertaken to achieve short-term, unilateral gains, perhaps even at the expense of a trading partner. As a result, opportunism by one party can erode the long-term gains potentially accruing to both parties in a relationship.

Because opportunism can be destructive to a business relationship, restraining opportunism is critical to enhancing performance and increasing mutual satisfaction.[1] Fortunately, mechanisms for managing opportunism in a marketing relationship exist.[2] Even before contracts are signed, business operators should carefully select their partners and design relationship agreements to discourage opportunistic behavior. Once a contract is signed, each party should monitor its partner's behavior to ensure mutual compliance.

The study presented in this chapter tested hypotheses pertaining to relationships in the hotel industry between individual hotels and their brand headquarters. On the one hand, corporate brands focus on developing and maintaining broad marketing programs that develop and market a brand identity. On the other hand, managers of individual hotel properties may be less than assiduous in fostering those brand identities. Hotel brands use a variety of mechanisms to govern individual properties' operations, including corporate ownership of each hotel (Red Roof Inns), franchise agreements (Holiday Inn), owning transaction-specific assets (reservation systems), and relational exchange (Choice Hotels' use of regional sales reps to assist its franchised hotels in developing marketing programs and implementing company-wide marketing programs).[3]

OPPORTUNISTIC BEHAVIOR

Much of the conceptual framework for controlling opportunistic behavior is grounded in *transaction cost analysis,* which provides a theoretical rationale for governance structures ranging from open markets (exchanges among independent producers and distributors) to hierarchies, in which many of the factors of production and distribution are owned in common. Franchising shares characteristics with both markets and hierarchies.

Opportunism has been characterized as "a lack of candor or honesty in transactions, to include self-interest seeking with guile."[4] Insofar as hotels operating under brand names put those names at risk, the brands rightly worry that their brand equity is at stake. Opportunistic behavior can potentially erode the brand's value.

Opportunism before the fact (adverse selection) occurs when one firm disguises its true ability to perform the functions required of the exchange. Hotel brands apply due diligence to prevent such opportunism. Franchise systems, for instance, carefully screen potential franchisees to eliminate property owners that are unlikely to maintain the hotel brand's quality image. Franchisees, on the other hand, attempt to verify independently the franchisor brand's revenue and profit projections. Parties in a prospective management agreement also make similar due diligence efforts before they sign a hotel management contract.

Opportunism can also occur after a relationship launches. Examples of such opportunism include withholding or distorting information so as to "mislead, distort, obfuscate, or otherwise confuse," or shirking duties, as in the case of "not delivering the promised action and resources, and failing to do this on a fairly systematic and sustained basis."[5] Hotel brands protect themselves against franchisee opportunism in some cases by establishing codes of ethical operation and setting up strict inspection systems.

MITIGATING OPPORTUNISM

This study viewed governance as "a multidimensional phenomenon which encompasses the initiation, termination, and ongoing relationship maintenance between a set of parties."[6] Governance mechanisms establish and structure exchange relationships. They differ, however, "in their capacities to respond effectively to disturbances [i.e., opportunism]."[7] Accordingly, the study examined the efficacy of three mechanisms for mitigating opportunism in hotel-marketing channels: (a) brand headquarters' ownership of a hotel, (b) investments made by a hotel in transaction-specific assets, and (c) relational-exchange norms developed between a hotel and its brand headquarters.

Ownership. According to transaction cost analysis, investments in transaction-specific assets are often best safeguarded through ownership, which enables the brand to manage its hotels' opportunistic tendencies in two ways.[8] First, ownership offers the potential for a richer system of rewards and punishment. Second, the organizational culture shared by headquarters and its hotels provides common norms and values that (should) align their interests.[9]

Ownership permits a brand to employ extensive monitoring and surveillance of its outlets. For example, from their headquarters brands have access to records, can conduct inspections, and can request reports necessary for evaluating a particular hotel's outcomes. Furthermore, a vertically integrated brand can use more subtle rewards with employees (assignments to desirable hotels) and more extensive sanctions (suspensions with or without pay) than it could apply to independent partners.[10] Most tellingly, ownership weakens all parties' incentives to behave opportunistically because it is impossible for any party to do so without ultimately hurting itself (as part of the company).[11]

Under common ownership, moreover, a brand and its hotels are likely to share a similar organizational culture and, thus, a consistent set of norms and values. Through common norms and values, a hotel's objectives become more closely aligned with the brand's objectives. Such alignment reduces hotel managers' incentives to behave opportunistically.

Given these considerations pertaining to brand headquarters' hotel ownership, the study's first hypothesis was that *hotel opportunism will be reduced where brand headquarters has full ownership of a hotel.*

Transaction-Specific Assets. Transaction-specific assets, which include specialized equipment and facilities as well as specialized training and experience, have little or no value outside of the exchange relationship.[12] For example, brand-affiliated hotels often invest in specific physical assets (furnishings, supplies, and signs) and idiosyncratic intangible assets (information systems, reservations systems, and management procedures) that could not easily be used if the hotel were to transfer to another brand.

Businesses invest in transaction-specific assets for at least three reasons. First, such assets are more efficient and effective than generalized assets in accomplishing business objectives. By investing in particular signs or computer software and giving employees specialized training, a hotel can appeal more effectively to its target market and serve that market more efficiently. Second, investing in transaction-specific assets signals a property's honorable intentions with respect to the trading relationship.[13] Third, such investments may be required as a condition of exchange, beyond the purposes of effectiveness and efficiency. In this instance, transaction-specific assets can be required essentially as performance bonds to be forfeited if a hotel is found to behave opportunistically.

All three motives for investing in transaction-specific assets—an explicit part of the performance-bonding motive—involve the potential for economic loss. If a partnership is terminated, a hotel can lose the full value of those assets (such as buildings constructed on land leased from the franchisor), its nonsalvageable value (brand-specific knowledge that cannot be redeployed to other exchange relationships), and the future income stream generated by the assets (a hotel's traffic generated by its brand's reservation system).[14]

Insofar as a firm's opportunistic behavior may be grounds for terminating a business relationship, several researchers have posited that the risk of forfeiting those idiosyncratic investments restrains hotel malfeasance.[15] Thus, the study's second hypothesis is *A hotel's opportunism will be reduced by its investments in transaction-specific assets.*

Relational Exchange. Relationships among firms can be characterized by exchange norms, such as role integrity, mutuality, solidarity, flexibility, information exchange, harmonious conflict resolution, and a long-term orientation.[16] Shared norms are characteristic of relational exchange, which is the final mechanism for managing opportunism that was investigated.[17] Some common components of relational exchange are defined below.

Relationship preservation is the extent to which channel members view their relationship as more than a series of discrete transactions, see the relationship as intrinsically valuable, and wish to preserve that relationship.[18] *Role integrity* entails channel members' expectations of needed future roles and suggests that roles expand to "cover a multitude of issues not directly related to any particular transaction."[19] This contractual norm ensures the stability necessary for deepening exchange relationships.[20] The abovementioned norm of *harmonization of relational conflict* refers to the extent to which channel members achieve mutually satisfying conflict resolution.[21] Because exchange norms indicate "relationalism," the study viewed the *extent of relational exchange* in a marketing channel as the degree to which the norms of role integrity, relationship preservation, and harmonization of relational conflict characterize that channel.[22]

Thus, relational exchange limits opportunism through common norms and values. By subscribing to a relationship-preservation norm, exchange partners see a relationship as ongoing and mutually beneficial and refrain from taking actions that jeopardize the relationship.[23] Based on those arguments, the study hypothesized that *opportunism will be reduced by perceived relational exchange between a hotel and its brand headquarters.*

The study also tested for interactions among the three methods of controlling opportunism to determine whether, for example, ownership combined with relational exchange had even greater influence than ownership alone, and so on.

The Study

The hypotheses were tested by examining relationships between individual hotels and their brand headquarters associated with two large hotel brands doing business in North America. The two brands were selected because they have both brand-owned properties and franchised units. In all, 368 general managers of hotels affiliated with these brands returned the questionnaire. Nonresponse bias checks yielded no significant evidence of such bias.

MEASURES

The role of opportunism was tested with questions pertaining to ten items; that of transaction-specific assets was tested with six items, and that of relational exchange was tested with fifteen items divided to account for role integrity, preservation of the relationship, and harmonization of conflict. Statistical tests demonstrated the reliability and validity of all measures.

OWNERSHIP

Every hotel's general manager was asked to indicate whether the hotel was wholly brand owned, was wholly independently owned, or had shared ownership. Shared-ownership properties were eliminated because there were so few of them (twenty-seven hotels). The analysis compared the 39 hotels that were wholly chain owned with the 329 properties that were wholly independently owned.

CONTROL VARIABLES

Two control variables were included. Every hotel in the sample was coded according to which of the two brands it represented. Hotel size was also controlled for, in case relationships with brand headquarters differed between large hotels and small hotels.

Results

Statistical analysis was applied to the hypotheses. Because interaction terms were included to represent combinations of governance mechanisms, the interaction effects were also analyzed. The analysis ruled out the control variables (brand affiliation and hotel size) as factors contributing to opportunism.

OWNERSHIP EFFECT

The first hypothesis was that brand headquarters' equity in a hotel would limit the hotel's opportunistic behavior. The analysis did not bear this out, indicating that when a brand owns a hotel it may be slightly more likely to behave opportunistically. Since this finding was not statistically significant, however, the study suggested at most that brand ownership of a hotel has no significant effect on hotel opportunism.

TRANSACTION-SPECIFIC ASSETS

The second hypothesis was that investing in transaction-specific assets reduces opportunistic behavior. Hotel-specific assets were isolated for the analysis through the assumption that hotels would be independently owned with minimal relational exchange with headquarters. Contrary to the hypothesis, the results implied that the more a hotel has invested in transaction-specific assets, the *more* likely it is to behave opportunistically. This finding indicates that a hotel's idiosyncratic assets exacerbate its opportunistic behavior in some way.

RELATIONAL EXCHANGE

The results suggested that the use of relational exchange as a governance mechanism indeed mitigates a hotel's opportunistic tendencies. This confirmed the hypothesis regarding relational exchange.

Combining Governance Mechanisms

In examining the simultaneous effect of the three governance mechanisms, it was assumed, consistent with transaction cost analysis, that ownership is the key governance alternative to the discipline of the marketplace.[24] Accordingly, the analysis was adjusted to reflect the assumption that a hotel's idiosyncratic investments and the extent of perceived relational exchange with its brand moderate the effects of brand ownership on hotel opportunism. Because the use of transaction-specific assets as a governance mechanism is also rooted in transaction cost analysis, it was assumed that a strong relationship moderates linkages between opportunism and transaction-specific assets.

Ownership and Transaction-Specific Assets. A moderate effect on opportunism resulting from a combination of brand ownership of a hotel and the hotel's investment in transaction-specific assets was found. This effect was not significant, however, providing no support for the hypothesis that a hotel's investment in specialized assets coupled with brand ownership reduces hotel opportunism.

Ownership and Relational Exchange. Regarding the hypothesis that higher degrees of relational exchange intensify the effect of brand ownership in lessening a hotel's opportunistic behavior, the results echoed those pertaining to ownership effects when isolated. Increasing levels of relational exchange along with brand ownership heightened, rather than reduced, hotel opportunism. Again, however, the differences among those effects were not statistically significant.

Transaction-Specific Assets and Relational Exchange. Finally, the results pertaining to the hypothesis that opportunistic behavior can be reduced by a combination of increasing idiosyncratic investments and greater perception of relational exchange with a brand suggested that changes in the level of relational exchange did not affect the relationship between opportunism and transaction-specific assets. Similarly, a combination of all three factors had no significantly greater effect on opportunism than did each one independently. In fact, increasing both hotel asset investment and relational exchange from moderate to high levels exacerbated rather than mitigated hotel opportunism.

A Relational-Exchange Perspective

Because transaction cost analysis has played a huge role in the study of marketing-channel governance, the study focused on the role of relational exchange in moderating the effects of transaction cost governance mechanisms (that is, the effects of ownership and idiosyncratic investments) on opportunistic behavior.

Turning that analysis around to look at how transaction cost mechanisms moderate the impact of relational exchange on hotel opportunism, the study then evaluated the change in opportunism with respect to the change in relationship quality, as mitigated by the other factors, namely, ownership and investment in specific assets.

The study found, for instance, that ownership has a significant influence on the effect of relational exchange on hotel opportunism and that brand ownership reduces opportunism in the presence of a good relationship. Assuming independent hotel ownership, the effect of increasing investment in specialized assets is to increase the influence of relational exchange in suppressing opportunism.

Ostensibly, the investigation of the impact of the simultaneous use of these governance mechanisms produced contradictory findings. Some of the results supported the hypotheses, while others did not. Although an analysis using the transaction cost approach generally did not support the hypotheses, application of a relational-exchange perspective did. It appears that in cases in which relational exchange is emphasized (either singly or in combination with idiosyncratic investments), hotel opportunism decreases. In cases in which either ownership or investments in specialized assets are stressed, hotel opportunism increases.

Actionable Insights

Reducing Opportunism

The strongest finding coming from this analysis is that a brand's managers should focus on building effective relationships with the general managers of their affiliated hotels. A strong relationship is the only governance mechanism that placed any significant limitation on hotel opportunism among the sampled hotels. Simply owning a hotel has no significant effect on its opportunistic actions, even when combined with the other governing mechanisms. Contrary to the predictions of transaction cost theory, the study suggests that increased investment in specialized assets can actually increase opportunism.

The results suggest that when brands aggressively exert ownership rights, opportunism can be exacerbated. Perhaps this is because ownership pressure and sanctions provoke GMs into exerting their independence—thus producing the opposite of the intended effect. Moreover, the extrinsic rewards available through hotel ownership may reduce a hotel manager's intrinsic motivation to cooperate, especially where norms of relational exchange are prevalent.[25]

In contrast, relational exchange depends on building common norms and values. A strong relationship leads to a sense of identification between a hotel and its brand. The hotel manager believes that whatever harms the brand also damages the hotel, and vice versa. The study suggests that this effect persists even when relational exchange is used in conjunction with ownership or investment in specialized assets. Apparently top management should emphasize building strong relationships to reduce opportunistic behavior at affiliated hotels.

RELATIONS OVER TRANSACTIONS

The finding that brand ownership of a hotel does little to limit the hotel's opportunism is inconsistent with transaction cost theory, as were the results regarding investments in transaction-specific assets. Perhaps the positive link between investment in specialized assets and opportunism is that opportunistic behavior helps the hotel generate additional returns on such investments.

To be sure, hotel brands may not regard transaction-specific assets as governance mechanisms. They may be more interested in the operational consistency gained by ownership in fostering the hotel's critical role of maintaining and reinforcing the brand's image. Additional research would be needed to test this supposition.

It is also possible that the hotel brands involved in the study performed poorly in using those assets for governance. When monitoring or punishments are ineffectual, the threat of economic losses rooted in a hotel's asset investment has little effect on opportunism. Further research is needed to investigate the effectiveness with which brands monitor their hotels and sanction them for opportunistic behavior.

Finally, the results revealed that relational exchange plays a central role in the operation of ownership and asset investment as governance mechanisms. The most effective governance mechanisms that we uncovered were the combination of ownership with relational exchange and asset investment with relational exchange. That is a departure from much of the channel-governance literature. This result suggests that the extent of relational exchange between channel partners is an important factor that must be considered before offering prescriptions based purely on transaction cost analysis.

1 Jule B. Gassenheimer, David B. Baucus, and Melissa S. Baucus, "Cooperative Arrangements among Entrepreneurs: An Analysis of Opportunism and Communication in Franchise Structures," *Journal of Business Research* 36, no. 1 (1996): 67–79.

2 Rodney L. Stump and Jan B. Heide, "Controlling Supplier Opportunism in Industrial Relationships," *Journal of Marketing Research* 33, no. 4 (1996): 431–41.

3 For a fuller discussion of these and other mechanisms used to govern vertical relationships in the hotel industry, see Chekitan S. Dev and James R. Brown, "Franchising and Other Operating Arrangements in the Lodging Industry: A Strategic Comparison," *Journal of Hospitality and Tourism Research* 14, no. 3 (1991): 25; Robert C. Lewis, Richard E. Chambers, and Harsha E. Chacko, *Marketing Leadership in Hospitality: Foundations and Practices,* 2nd ed. (New York: Van Nostrand Reinhold, 1995), 650–80; and Mike Malley, "Getting the Most Value out of Franchising," *Hotel and Motel Management* (supplement) 212, no. 8 (1997): 31–32.

4 Oliver E. Williamson, *The Economic Institutions of Capitalism—Firms, Markets, Relational Contracting* (New York: Free Press, 1985), 9.

5 Ibid., 47; Kenneth G. Hardy and Alan J. Magrath, "Dealing with Cheating in Distribution," *European Journal of Marketing* 23, no. 2 (1989): 123.

6 Gassenheimer, Baucus, and Baucus, "Cooperative Arrangements among Entrepreneurs," 72.

7 Williamson, *The Economic Institutions of Capitalism,* 45.

8 Ibid., 56–57.

9 See George John and Barton A. Weitz, "Forward Integration into Distribution: An Empirical Test of Transaction Cost Analysis," *Journal of Law, Economics, and Organization,* 4, no. 2 (1988): 337–55.

10 Erin Anderson and Barton A. Weitz, "Make-or-Buy Decisions: Vertical Integration and Marketing Productivity," *Sloan Management Review* 27, no. 3 (1986): 3–19.

11 Oliver E. Williamson, *Markets and Hierarchies: Analysis and Anti-trust Implications* (New York: Free Press, 1975).

12 Anderson and Weitz, "Make-or-Buy Decisions"; Williamson, *The Economic Institutions of Capitalism,* 55; Ritu Lohita, Charles M. Brooks, and Robert E. Krapfel, "What Constitutes a Transaction-Specific Asset? An Examination of the Dimensions and Types," *Journal of Business Research* 30, no. 3 (1994): 261–70.

13 Debi Pradad Mishra, Jan B. Heide, and Stanton G. Cort, "Information Asymmetry and Levels of Agency Relationships," *Journal of Marketing Research* 35, no. 3 (1998): 277–95.

14 Paul Rubin, *Managing Business Transactions* (New York: Free Press, 1990).

15 Among them are Stump and Heide, "Controlling Supplier Opportunism in Industrial Relationships," 431–41.

16 See Patrick J. Kaufmann and Louis W. Stern, "Relational Exchange Norms, Perceptions of Unfairness, and Retained Hostility in Commercial Litigation," *Journal of Conflict Resolution* 32, no. 3 (1988): 534–52; Patrick J. Kaufmann and Rajiv P. Dant, "The Dimensions of Commercial Exchange," *Marketing Letters* 3, no. 2 (1992): 171–85; and Shankar S. Ganesan, "Determinants of Long-Term Orientation in Buyer-Seller Relationships," *Journal of Marketing* 58, no. 2 (1994): 1–19.

17 See Jan B. Heide and George John, "Do Norms Matter in Marketing Relationships?" *Journal of Marketing* 56, no. 2 (1992): 32–44; Ian R. Macneil, *The New Social Contract* (New Haven, CT: Yale University Press, 1980); and F. Robert Dwyer, Paul F. Schurr, and Sejo Oh, "Developing Buyer-Seller Relationships," *Journal of Marketing* 51, no. 2 (1987): 11–27.

18 See Macneil, *The New Social Contract;* and Kaufmann and Stern, "Relational Exchange Norms," 534–52.

19 Ibid., 536.

20 See Rajiv P. Dant and Patrick L. Schul, "Conflict Resolution Processes in Contractual Channels of Distribution," *Journal of Marketing* 56, no. 1 (1992): 43; and Kaufmann and Dant, "The Dimensions of Commercial Exchange."

21 Macneil, *The New Social Contract.*

22 See Thomas G. Noordwier, George John, and John R. Nevin, "Performance Outcomes of Purchasing Arrangements in Industrial Buyer-Vendor Relationships," *Journal of Marketing* 54, no. 4 (1990): 80–93; and Heide and John, "Do Norms Matter in Marketing Relationships?," 32–44.

23 See Victor P. Goldberg, "Relational Exchange: Economics and Complex Contracts," *American Behavioral Scientist* 23, no. 3 (1980): 337–52; Paul L. Joskow, "Contract Duration and Relationship-Specific Investments: Empirical Evidence from Coal Markets," *American Economic Review* 77, no. 1 (1987): 168–85; Jan B. Heide and George John, "Alliances in Industrial Purchasing: The Determinants of Joint Action in Buyer-Supplier Relationships," *Journal of Marketing Research* 27, no. 1 (1990): 24–36; and Ganesan, "Determinants of Long-Term Orientation."

24 See Williamson, *Markets and Hierarchies.*

25 Compare to Bruno S. Frey, "Does Monitoring Increase Work Effort? The Rivalry with Trust and Loyalty," *Economic Inquiry* 31, no. 4 (1993): 663–70.

CHAPTER ELEVEN

Brand Franchising

The importance of franchising to the development of the U.S. lodging and restaurant industries cannot be overstated. Franchising was, for example, the vehicle for the initial expansion of Holiday Inn and McDonalds in the 1950s. In recent years franchising has been an expansion strategy employed by hotel and restaurant brands in many segments. For example, according to industry analyst Stephen Rushmore, "Franchised hotels account for more than 65 percent of the existing U.S. hotel-room supply."[1] As franchising increases its share of the lodging and restaurant industries, achieving higher levels of market growth becomes more difficult for the franchisors. Lately researchers have been investigating a new tool for gaining competitive advantage that falls under the generic name of *relationship marketing*. This involves strengthening a brand's relationships with its suppliers and customers.[2] This chapter presents a study that was conducted to capture insights that could be applied in improving the franchisor-franchisee relationship in the hospitality industry.

The Challenge

The primary customers for hotel franchisors are their franchisees. Consequently, the relationship between a franchisor and the franchisees that are responsible for operating the hotels bearing a franchisor brand's flag is especially critical. Local franchisees put into practice the plans and strategies formulated by the brand. Moreover, the local operators are responsible for managing direct contact with the brand's ultimate customers, the guests.

Effective relationships between hotel franchisors and their franchised hotels are truly partnerships—relationships that benefit both parties. Not only do both the hotel and the brand benefit from a partnership arrangement; both also have a meaningful say regarding the strategic direction the partnership takes. Increasing mutual participation in the decision-making process gives partners an expanded stake in the success of the relationship and encourages them to work harder to ensure that success. As a result, building marketing partnerships between hotel franchisors and their franchisees should lead to stronger performance.

This proposition was explored in this study by asking the following question: *Does a stronger marketing partnership between a hotel franchisor and its franchised hotel lead to higher performance, both for the hotel and for the partnership as a whole?*

The answer to this research question was pursued by surveying hotel general managers at properties affiliated with two major U.S. brands. This chapter discusses the notion of marketing partnerships, informs that discussion with traditional views of economic exchange, and clarifies what *higher performance* means. The chapter concludes by explaining the results of the study and summarizing the resulting insights.

DISCRETE AND COMPLEX EXCHANGES

Traditional economic theory views relationships among independent businesses as short-term exchanges that are terminated at the conclusion of transactions. Suppose the car of a traveling salesperson has broken down and he or she has to spend the night at an unfamiliar mom-and-pop motel in a strange town. The salesperson has no intention of returning to the motel once the car is fixed and is ready to move on his or her way to the next sales call. The terms of such short-term exchanges are simple—money is exchanged for the service of a room for the night. Neither the seller nor the buyer has any expectations that a long-term relationship will develop from such an exchange. Such one-shot, arm's-length relationships between buyers and sellers are termed *discrete exchanges.*[3] While many transactions are discrete exchanges, the contemporary marketplace usually involves exchanges of greater complexity, involving implied or express agreements and contracts.[4] The multitude of frequent-guest programs, buyers' clubs, and affinity credit cards on the market demonstrates retailers' efforts to extend such trading beyond discrete exchanges.

Firms involved in complex exchanges behave more like partners and less like purveyors and customers conducting an arm's-length business transaction. These partnerships last longer, are more personal, and are more intertwined than discrete exchanges are—and they often involve explicit contracts. For example, because their franchise contracts can last up to twenty years, Holiday Inn and its franchisees are bound to each other for more than just a single transaction. Such long-term exchanges become personal as, for instance, the brand's field representative calls upon the same hotel managers time after time. This enables people in both the brand and the hotel to develop personal rapport.

Marketing Partnerships

The partnership concept assumes that success depends on the success of all involved business associates. Certainly that is the case in the lodging industry. An individual hotel would have difficulty succeeding as a member of a weak brand, although local conditions sometimes allow that to occur. Similarly, a hotel brand comprising weak local operations will struggle, no matter how excellent its concept.

Moreover, brands and hotels in effective marketing partnerships jointly plan to attain mutual goals and objectives. Among the factors that are critical in guiding such joint planning are (a) the mutual desire to preserve the relationship, (b) role integrity, and (c) the harmonization of marketing conflict.[5]

The mutual desire to preserve a relationship is based on the extent to which the parties view that relationship as richer than a series of discrete transactions. It also depends on the extent to which the parties agree that the relationship is intrinsically important and the extent to which the partners view themselves as members of the same team.[6]

A contract defines the goods or services that each firm provides to the partnership and what each can expect to gain. Beyond that, roles in relational partnerships "cover a multitude of issues not directly related to any particular transaction."[7]

Role integrity is achieved in a relationship when all parties clearly understand their respective rights and responsibilities. The more clearly these roles are understood by all, the easier it is for partners to predict how each will behave and the more smoothly the relationship will operate. Role integrity is critical to providing the stability necessary to allow exchange relationships to deepen.[8] This characteristic encourages partners to make decisions and behave in ways that strengthen a relationship.

Enduring relationships of all types experience difficulties. Relational partnerships survive these difficulties because the parties attempt to resolve their conflicts in mutually satisfying ways. In the harmonizing of relational conflict, the integrity of a partnership is placed above the separate interests of the individual parties.[9]

Franchisor-Franchisee Performance

In franchising there are three objects of performance evaluation: the franchisee, the franchisor, and the franchisor-franchisee relationship. The study presented here investigated two of these: how well a partnership performs and how well a hotel performs. To judge how well a hotel-franchisor relationship performed overall, the study relied on the judgment of the hotel general managers.

For the purposes of the study, franchisee performance was treated as a financial measure, reflecting both common sense and previous research.[10] This entailed investigating hotel sales volume and profitability in terms of both gross operating profit and net operating profit.[11] A hotel's competitive performance against its direct competitors was also investigated and compared with that of other hotels of the same brand. These comparisons were based on occupancy rate, average room rate, gross operating profit, quality assurance evaluations, and guest satisfaction ratings.[12]

To test whether strong relationships lead to higher performance, the relationships of two major hotel franchisors with their individual North American hotel properties were examined. The analysis was based on survey questionnaires returned by 331 general managers, representing an acceptable response rate. Nonresponse bias was ruled out.

Measurements

Scoring Partnerships. Because an effective marketing partnership rests on the three distinct dimensions of preservation of the relationship, role integrity, and harmonization of conflict, hotel general managers were asked to rate their relationships with brand headquarters on each of these three dimensions, using fourteen questionnaire items. According to the usual rules of interpretation, analysis showed that the marketing partnership scale was indeed reliable and valid. The sample was then divided into thirds based on the marketing-partnership scores, which were classified as low, moderate, and strong.

Checking the Relationship. The general managers responded to four questions to assess the overall performance of their relationships.[13] The responses were then averaged to obtain a measure of overall performance of a hotel-franchisor relationship. The reliability and validity of this measure was then affirmed.

A hotel's competitive performance reflects its ability to support its franchisor's efforts in the hotel's local market. Each hotel's general manager was asked to compare his or her hotel's performance with that of its direct competitors on three key operating measures—occupancy rate, average daily rate (ADR), and gross operating profit (GOP).

Each general manager also compared his or her hotel with other hotels of the same brand on quality assurance ratings and guest satisfaction ratings, both of which scores were treated as a separate measure.

Financial performance was measured by three key indicators—sales revenue, GOP, and income before fixed costs—expressed per available room (RevPAR, gross operating profit per available room [GOPPAR], and income before fixed charges per available room [IBFCPAR]) and per available employee (revenue per employee [REVEMP], gross operating profit per employee [GOPEMP], and income before fixed charges per employee [IBFCEMP]). The performance measures were adjusted in this way to eliminate distortions caused by hotel size.

The per-available-room and per-available-employee standards put hotels on relatively equal footing. Moreover, assessing financial performance in terms of rooms available and number of employees indicated how effectively a hotel used its resources—physical capital and labor—to generate sales revenues and profits. The higher the sales revenues per room were (and, hence, the higher the franchise royalty fees), the happier was the franchisor. The higher the profits were, the happier the hotel owner was.

Results

After the overall performance of franchisor-franchisee relationships were tested, the findings indicated that a relationship's overall performance does indeed vary significantly according to its partnership score. Additional testing showed that higher relationship performance is associated with stronger marketing partnerships. Thus, the more a hotel and its brand headquarters worked as a team (in the general manager's view), the better was the partnership's overall performance. This result was consistent with the research proposition.

In terms of competitive performance, the results indicated that, compared with those of its direct competitors, when a hotel's management and its franchisor scored high in acting as partners, the occupancy rate, the average room rate, and (consequently) gross operating profits were also higher. When general managers assessed other hotels of the same brand, the results showed that as a hotel's partnership score increases, so do its quality assurance and guest satisfaction ratings. Taken together, these results were also consistent with the overall research proposition: stronger partnerships between franchised hotels and their brand headquarters lead to better performance on both sides of a partnership.

Hotel financial performance was then compared across the three groupings by partnership score (low, moderate, and strong). The results showed that hotel financial performance generally does improve as a hotel and its franchisor work more closely together. GOPPAR was higher, on average, for the medium and strong marketing-partnership groups than for the weakest group. IBFCPAR was significantly greater for strong hotel-franchisor partnerships. Although sales revenue per available room appeared to differ across the three groups, these differences were not statistically significant. Thus, the stronger the hotel-headquarters partnership was, the more the hotel was able to generate both GOP as well as net profits from its available rooms. This finding was consistent with the research proposition.

Employee productivity paralleled room productivity. The strength of the hotel-franchisor partnership had no significant bearing on REVEMP or GOPEMP. Stronger partnerships did, however, generate greater net operating profits per employee (IBFCEMP). This finding was consistent with overall expectations.

Actionable Insights

The results of the study presented in this chapter indicate that, if a franchisor wants to improve the performance of its hotels, it should treat them more like partners than as "necessary evils" to be tolerated or, worse, as adversaries to exploit.

The study clearly shows the manifold benefits of strong marketing partnerships:

- Higher overall performance of the hotel-franchisor relationship
- Higher hotel occupancy rates than the direct competition's
- Higher average room rates than the direct competition's
- Higher gross operating profits than the direct competition's
- Higher quality assurance ratings than those of other hotels under the brand
- Higher guest satisfaction ratings than those of other hotels under the brand
- Higher GOP earnings and income before interest and taxes (in terms of available rooms) than those of hotels with weaker partnerships
- Higher income before fixed costs (on a per employee basis) than those of hotels with weaker partnerships.

Some franchisors clearly understand the importance of working closely with their franchisees. For example, Courtyard by Marriott encourages its franchisees to participate in its support and service programs. This strengthens the franchisor-franchisee relationship. As Craig Lambert, the chain's brand vice president, observed, "The more [franchisees] are involved, the better the outcome."[14] In view of the study's findings, it is surprising that more franchisors do not strengthen their partnerships with their hotels.

The research suggests several ways in which a brand can strengthen its hotel partnerships: First, franchisor brands should view relationships with their hotels as intrinsically important and they should genuinely strive to preserve those relationships. Second, franchisor brands should behave in a stable fashion by refraining from abrupt and frequent changes in strategic direction that confuse and frustrate franchisees. Third, franchisor brands and franchisees should jointly form clear expectations about what functions each is to perform and how that performance is to be evaluated by the brand. Similarly, hotels must have clear expectations about the support that they can receive from a franchisor. Feedback programs that allow hotels to evaluate franchisor brand performance along dimensions that affect it are also important. Finally, franchisor brands and hotels should work in a harmonious way to resolve the inevitable conflicts that arise in any business relationship. This means ensuring that all parties' concerns are resolved to their mutual satisfaction. When all parties are satisfied, a relationship becomes team oriented instead of adversary oriented.

In addition, it is important to exercise power judiciously. For example, in his study of franchise relationships in the quick-service-restaurant industry, H. G. Parsa found franchisees to be more satisfied when franchisors relied on legitimate authority, relationship bonds, and high-quality information and support.[15] He also found franchisees to be more satisfied when franchisors avoided relying on coercion to influence their franchisees. There is no reason to think that the use of power in lodging-industry franchise relationships should operate differently.

Other researchers suggest additional dimensions of marketing partnerships, although they were not included in this study. These include flexibility on the part of brands and hotels in dealing with one another, mutual sharing of information, and adopting a long-term orientation to a relationship.[16] Also critical to effective marketing partnerships are mutual trust and commitment, fair treatment and just outcomes, and mutual interdependency.[17] A partnership that stresses these qualities should expect its performance to increase commensurately.

The Growth Factor

Hotel franchisors court additional franchisees as marketing partners for continued growth in sales revenue. In today's competitive climate, potential franchisees, especially those with lots of promise, have their choice of suitors and are likely to scrutinize them carefully. As this research made clear, hotels affiliated with brands that forge strong partnerships are more likely to achieve superior performance. A brand that promises (and delivers) strong partnerships is more likely to have its choice of prospective hotel partners. Thus, developing strong partnerships can be a powerful tool that franchisors can use to recruit high-quality franchisees.

If hotels wish to experience the benefits of a strong hotel-brand partnership, they must be willing to work on behalf of the partnership, perform roles that extend beyond their traditional boundaries, and resolve their disagreements to the benefit of the partnership rather than to their own benefit. In short, strong partnerships require sacrifices on the part of both a hotel and its brand. The research presented in this chapter shows, however, that such sacrifices yield substantial payoffs in terms of hotel performance as well as the performance of the relationship as a whole.

---

1 Stephen Rushmore, "Hotel Franchising: How to Be a Successful Franchisee," *Real Estate Journal,* Summer 1997, 56.

2 F. Robert Dwyer, Paul F. Schurr, and Sejo Oh, "Developing Buyer-Seller Relationships," *Journal of Marketing* 51, no. 2 (1987): 11–27; and Jan B. Heide, "Interorganizational Governance in Marketing Channels," *Journal of Marketing* 58, no. 1 (1994): 71–85.

3 For a discussion of the characteristics of discrete exchange, see Dwyer, Schurr, and Oh, "Developing Buyer-Seller Relationships," table 1, 13.

4 See Johan Arndt, "Toward a Concept of Domesticated Markets," *Journal of Marketing* 43, no. 4 (1979): 69–75.

5 Ian R. Macneil, *The New Social Contract* (New Haven, CT: Yale University Press, 1980), 65.

6 See Macneil, *The New Social Contract;* and Patrick J. Kaufmann and Louis W. Stern, "Relational Exchange Norms, Perceptions of Unfairness, and Retained Hostility in Commercial Litigation," *Journal of Conflict Resolution* 32, no. 3 (1988): 534–52.

7 Kaufmann and Stern, "Relational Exchange Norms," 536.

8 Rajiv P. Dant and Patrick L. Schul, "Conflict Resolution Processes in Contractual Channels of Distribution," *Journal of Marketing* 56, no. 1 (1992): 43.

9 Macneil, *The New Social Contract,* 68

10 See, for example, Chekitan S. Dev and James R. Brown, "Marketing Strategy, Vertical Structure, and Performance in the Lodging Industry: A Contingency Approach," *International Journal of Hospitality Management* 9, no. 3 (1990): 269–82.

11 Robert C. Lewis and Richard E. Chambers, *Marketing Leadership in Hospitality: Foundations and Practices* (New York: Van Nostrand Reinhold, 1989), 498–99.

12 Compare with Lewis and Chambers, *Marketing Leadership in Hospitality,* 498–99, 550, and 604.

13 These questionnaire items were based on the work of Nirmalya Kumar, Louis W. Stern, and Ravi S. Achrol, "Assessing Reseller Performance from the Perspective of the Supplier," *Journal of Marketing Research* 29, no. 2 (1992): 238–53.

14 Mike Malley, "Getting the Most Value out of Franchising," *Hotel and Motel Management* (supplement) 212, no. 8 (1997): 31–32.

15 H. G. Parsa, "Franchisor-Franchisee Relationships in Quick-Service-Restaurant Systems," *Cornell Hotel and Restaurant Administration Quarterly* 37, no. 3 (1996), 42–49.

16 See Patrick J. Kaufmann and Rajiv P. Dant, "The Dimensions of Commercial Exchange," *Marketing Letters* 3, no. 2 (1992): 171–85; Brett Boyle, F. Robert Dwyer, Robert A. Robicheaux, and James T. Simpson, "Influence Strategies in Marketing Channels: Measures and Use in Different Relationship Structures," *Journal of Marketing Research* 29, no. 4 (1992): 462–73; Jan B. Heide and George John, "Do Norms Matter in Marketing Relationships?" *Journal of Marketing* 56, no. 2 (1992): 32–44; and Thomas G. Noordwier, George John, and John R. Nevin, "Performance Outcomes of Purchasing Arrangements in Industrial Buyer-Vendor Relationships," *Journal of Marketing* 54, no. 4 (1990): 80–93.

17 Robert M. Morgan and Shelby D. Hunt, "The Commitment-Trust Theory of Relationship Marketing," *Journal of Marketing* 58, no. 3 (1994): 20–28; Nirmalya Kumar and Lisa K. Scheer, "The Effects of Supplier Fairness on Vulnerable Resellers," *Journal of Marketing Research* 32, no. 1 (1995): 54–65. See Robert F. Lusch and James R. Brown, "Interdependency, Contracting, and Relational Behavior in Marketing Channels," *Journal of Marketing* 60, no. 4 (1996): 19–38; and Nirmalya Kumar and Lisa K. Scheer, "The Effects of Perceived Interdependence on Dealer Attitudes," *Journal of Marketing Research* 32, no. 3 (1995): 348–56.

CHAPTER TWELVE

Brand Partnerships

Brand partnerships in hotels typically involve an owner (often a brand franchisee) and an operator (not always providing a brand identity), two separate business entities, both of which contribute their respective assets to give the hotel the required cachet to succeed in the marketplace. When their relationship is amicable, the two entities can work together to help the hotel project an attractive image and position itself against competing brands. The quality of such a brand partnership drives how customers, competitors, suppliers, and partners perceive the hotel. However, when the relationship is not cordial, one partner or the other might work deceptively in a self-interested pursuit of advantage. This chapter presents a study of that possibility, called *opportunism,* and discusses strategies for successful brand partnerships.

The Challenge

Many studies have concluded that good brand-partner relationships can create value for both parties. Positive brand partnerships reduce opportunism and increase mutual cooperation.[1] Moreover, better brand-hotel relationships lead to higher occupancy, average room rates, gross operating profits, quality assurance scores, and guest satisfaction ratings. Poor brand partnerships, on the other hand, have the opposite effect.[2] Let's look at two actual cases involving situations in which a hotel and its brand parted company.

Case Study 1

When Scott Robinson "did the math," his calculations changed not only the name of the downtown Toledo Ramada Inn and Suites hotel but also its business model. As general manager of the nineteen-story hotel, Robinson figured the property could do as much business as ever while saving thousands of dollars by severing ties with Ramada and selling rooms through the Internet as an independent. It would operate its own website and rent rooms at discount rates through online travel agents. "The individual hotel owners are caught in the middle of the battle between the chains and the web sites," he said. As a result, some hotel owners and managers, like Robinson, wonder whether they are better off without their brand affiliations. Cutting ties with Ramada saved the newly christened Hotel Seagate $212,000 a year in franchise and marketing fees.[3]

CASE STUDY 2

Innkeepers USA Trust, a hotel real estate investment trust and a leading owner of upscale, extended-stay hotel properties, announced that it had completed the acquisition of the 182-room Clarion Hotel in downtown Louisville, for $6.4 million. The property, which was in foreclosure, would be repositioned and converted to a Hampton Inn following a $4.5 million renovation program. "Hampton is one of the strongest brands in the industry and offers guests all the advantages of the Hilton family of hotel brands, including HHonors, Hilton's award-winning frequent guest program, and access to Hilton's worldwide reservations system," say the new owners.[4]

MANAGING BRAND PARTNERSHIPS

These case studies illustrate the costs of a failed relationship between a hotel and its brand. In both cases, a brand lost its market presence, and in the second case the hotel owner had also lost the investment to foreclosure. Smith Travel Research reports that thousands of hotels change brand affiliations every year. Managing these brand relations well has become a top priority for brands and hotels alike.

Opportunism occurs when one partner acts dishonestly in its own interest. Although it is possible for parent brands to act opportunistically, the study presented in this chapter was concerned mainly with how such brands can influence the behavior of hotel-owning partners who try to take advantage of the relationship. The temptation to behave opportunistically arises in an environment in which, for their part, owners and managers want their hotels to be profitable (regardless of occupancy and rate), while, for their part, brands want to preserve their brand positioning. Brands therefore try to maintain their rates (sometimes at the cost of occupancy) and top-line revenue (sometimes at the cost of profit), as they typically are paid a percentage of that revenue. There is, then, a fundamental tension between rate and occupancy, on the one hand, and, on the other, revenue and profit (which can pit the owner's interests against the brands' interests). Thus, partners may be tempted to gain some advantage through dishonesty. For brand managers, understanding how to influence a partner's behavior in a way that minimizes opportunism not only can protect the brand's interests; it also can strengthen the hotel's business insofar as opportunism's short-term benefits often lead to long-term disadvantages for both partners.[5]

The purpose of this study was to test several strategies for managing brand partnerships to see which work best under a range of relationship conditions. In particular, the question was whether brands could manage opportunism better by forming relationships with their partners that established certain expectations or norms of behavior.

STUDYING OPPORTUNISM

This was among the few studies to investigate brand partnerships in the hospitality sector. Scholars have been studying opportunism more generally since the early 1980s, focusing on a variety of *influence strategies,* or means of communication that are expected to produce favorable outcomes, such as reduced intrabrand conflict, brand partner satisfaction, and loyalty.[6]

Scholars generally classify influence strategies as *coercive* or *noncoercive.* Coercive strategies are designed to control opportunism through some combination of rewards and punishments and by communicating to partners the likely consequences of guileful behavior. Here the basis for behaving cooperatively rather than antagonistically is said to be external to the target partner—the opportunistic behavior is altered not by making it less intrinsically attractive but rather by promising rewards for good behavior and threatening punishments for bad. Both rewards and punishments increase the net costs of opportunism. Even if the motive to behave opportunistically remains, the behavior is suppressed. The coercive strategies considered in the study included *promises, threats,* and *legalistic pleas.*

Noncoercive strategies attempt to change a brand partner's attitudes toward the partnership by influencing the target partner internally. Instead of discouraging opportunism directly, noncoercive strategies aim to make the target partner less disposed to opportunism. The three main categories of noncoercive influence strategies considered in the study were *information exchange, recommendations,* and *requests.*[7]

Scholars refer to the cultivation of relationships with brand partners that influence partner exchanges as *socialization*. Through socialization one partner hopes to align the goals of another partner with its own, thereby avoiding potential opportunism by establishing *relational norms* that make the second partner to some extent self-governing rather than responding only to more direct forms of influence. Such relational norms establish mutual expectations about appropriate behavior on the part of brand partners. This study focused on the following three norms that become especially salient in the context of close partner relationships: *solidarity, role integrity,* and *conflict harmonization.* When partners share the solidarity norm, they attach an intrinsic value to their partnership and pursue shared goals, sometimes even at the expense of self-interest. Partners that value role integrity share an interest in maintaining each other's contribution to the effectiveness of the partnership. Conflict harmonization indicates the extent to which partners are consistently able to resolve potential or actual conflicts quickly to their mutual satisfaction.[8]

CONCEPTUAL FRAMEWORK

While the scholarly literature has focused primarily on the direct effects of relational norms on opportunism, this study adopted a slightly more complex approach by examining whether relational norms play a moderating role with respect to influence strategies in limiting opportunism. The questions were whether and how socialization might enhance or inhibit the effectiveness of both coercive and noncoercive strategies. The idea was to yield implications for brand partners who are mindful of the level of socialization in their partnerships.

Noncoercive Strategies. Noncoercive strategies operate by affecting the attitudes and beliefs of a brand partner to become more supportive and cooperative. Some scholars have argued that relational norms may support this process by enhancing reciprocal communication between partners, making it easier for one partner to deliver a message that limits opportunism by disposing the other partner to fully and diligently process the information contained in the message. Within such an environment, noncoercive influence strategies can be applied more effectively to limit a partner's opportunism.[9]

Clearly such an environment should enhance the relational norms of role integrity and conflict harmonization. Effective message communication should encourage one's partner to fully process a message's content, and this helps to maintain the partners' respective roles. With open lines of communication the partners will have already overcome a barrier to conflict resolution, as their messages to and from one another will be conveyed clearly, facilitating negotiations over potential disagreements. When it is difficult for partners to communicate openly, by contrast, disputes arise over the messages themselves, blocking progress on more substantive issues such as price or supply availability. This renders noncoercive strategies ineffective, at best, and the relationship can deteriorate even further, as weak relational norms open communications to misinterpretations and eventually the exploitation of shared information.

Coercive Strategies. To fully investigate the impact of relational norms, however, it is necessary to focus also on coercive strategies, such as threats, promises, or appeals to legal obligations. In essence, coercive strategies invoke immediate rewards for complying with contractual agreements or exchange arrangements and punishments for noncompliance. This suggests that coercive strategies are only as effective as the credibility of the rewards and punishments being invoked. Because coercive strategies by design operate in the short term, they are likely to be most effective in an exchange environment in which the partners work at arm's length. If neither partner operates with long-term future outcomes in mind, imminent rewards and punishments seem more credible in the context of a relationship built on short-term financial outcomes.

Indeed, in an exchange environment characterized by strong relational norms, coercive strategies seem likely to provoke dismay and frustration. The perception that one's partner is seeking an untoward advantage easily justifies opportunistic behavior in reaction. It seems therefore that where strong relational norms prevail, norm violation is likely to be reciprocated. Coercive strategies work best when transactions are viewed as "strictly business," while noncoercive strategies work best when "It's a pleasure doing business with you" is a natural expression of partner commitment.[10]

HYPOTHESES

The effects of relational norms on influence strategies were tested by formulating four hypotheses, two in reference to noncoercive influence, and two in reference to coercive influence, as applied by hotel brands in their relationships with their hotels. The quality of the relationships was determined by ascertaining how the hotel managers perceived the role of relational norms in those partnerships.

Noncoercive Influence. Strong relational norms should make noncoercive influence more effective in limiting partner opportunism. If a hotel perceives that its relationship with a particular brand partner is based on strong relational norms, noncoercive influence will be more effective in limiting the hotel's opportunistic behavior. In other words, noncoercive influence works more effectively in limiting partner opportunism when a hotel's relationship with its brand is based on relational norms such as solidarity, role integrity, or conflict harmonization.

The converse of this hypothesis is that a partnership with weak relational norms will undermine the effectiveness of noncoercive strategies in limiting hotel opportunism. That is, the use of noncoercive techniques by brands will fail to limit opportunism on the part of hotels where relational norms are weak. Under these circumstances such approaches will likely increase opportunism when a property suspects the noncoercive approach or views it as indicating vulnerability.

Coercive Influence. Weak relational norms should enhance the effectiveness of coercive influence strategies in limiting opportunism on the part of hotels. That is, when strong relational norms have not developed in a partnership between a brand and a hotel, coercive strategies such as threats, promises, and legal pleas will be more effective in limiting the hotel's opportunism.

Conversely, when the partnership between a brand and a hotel features strong relational norms, the brand will be frustrated in its efforts to limit partner opportunism if it attempts to use coercive influence strategies. Here the hotel is likely to be surprised and dismayed by such coercive tactics—perhaps feeling that established norms have been violated—and is therefore more likely to consider retaliatory opportunism.

The Study

THE SAMPLE

These hypotheses were tested by examining the relationship between individual hotels and brand headquarters of two large hotel brands in North America, both of which include brand-owned hotels and franchised units in their portfolios. The data was based on a survey of 367 hotel general managers. No difference was found in the results between brands, and nonresponse bias was not an issue for the research.

MEASURES

Four constructs were selected to represent the factors to measure in testing the hypotheses: *hotel opportunism, brand headquarters' use of coercive influence, brand headquarters' use of noncoercive influence,* and *relational norms.* Hotel opportunism was measured as "active opportunism," which involves behaviors that are prohibited under the terms of a partner contract. The two categories of influence strategies were measured by targeting a set of component strategies for each one. Coercive influence was measured by inquiring about promises, threats, and legalistic pleas. Noncoercive influence was tested by inquiring about information exchange, recommendations, and requests. Relational norms were tested by measuring relationship preservation (solidarity), role integrity, and conflict harmonization, to determine the extent to which the sample of general managers applied these terms to their brand relationships.[11]

There were three control variables in the study. First, opportunism appears to be significantly related to dependence in relationships between partners, and the control for this factor involved motivational investment in the brand partner and the difficulty of brand replacement. Also, because the sample came from two brands and included both franchised and brand-owned properties, two control variables were added to account for these differences.[12]

Following factor analysis there was some adjustment that made it possible to combine items pertaining to the three individual relational norms into a single indicator of relational norms, and to combine two of the aspects of coercive influence (legalistic pleas and threats) into a single measure. The request strategy was excluded from the noncoercive influence category because it is rarely employed.[13] Following these adjustments, statistical tests confirmed the validity of all measures and ruled out common method bias.

Results

Analysis of the survey responses confirmed the two hypotheses pertaining to the use of noncoercive influence to limit partner opportunism. When brand relationships operated with strong relational norms, noncoercive influence effectively limited partner opportunism. Conversely, when relational norms were weak, noncoercive influence exacerbated partner opportunism. That is, when a brand employs noncoercive influence strategies in the presence of strong relational norms, opportunism decreases, whereas it increases when the brand applies noncoercive strategies in the presence of weak relational norms.

Mixed results were found regarding coercive influence strategies. The first hypothesis, which predicted that brand relationships characterized by weak relational norms would enable coercive influence to effectively limit partner opportunism, was not confirmed. Based on the study's findings, coercive strategies were linked to an increase in opportunism even when employed in the presence of weak relational norms. On the other hand, the second hypothesis about coercive influence was confirmed by the survey responses, according to which, when relational norms were strong, coercive influence exacerbated partner opportunism. That is, when a brand employed coercive strategies in the presence of strong relational norms, opportunism increased significantly. In short, coercive strategies are correlated with an increase in opportunism regardless of the status of the relationship. Still, coercion provoked less opportunism in a weak relationship than in a strong one, suggesting that coercive tactics are somewhat less damaging when relational norms are weak than when they are strong.

Actionable Insights

Before reviewing the practical insights from this study, it must be noted that the data were based on the perceptions reported by hotel managers of their brand partnerships rather than on the perceptions of brand executives. It is certainly possible that brand executives would not have perceived such partnerships precisely as their hotel managers did. The study also clearly identified an area that deserves further research, namely, the question of how relational norms are developed and preserved.

Based on what the study says about hotel managers' perceptions, however, brand executives should approach opportunism on the part of hotels by carefully assessing the quality of their relationships. Those who enjoy relatively close relationships marked by strong relational norms, such as solidarity and conflict harmonization, should find it advantageous to employ noncoercive influence strategies in trying to limit or prevent opportunism. They can expect that, when they share information with hotels, the hotels will not misuse that information and that they can rely on the information that flows back from the hotels. The study showed that if you are a brand executive, the better your relationship with your hotels is, the more effective noncoercive influence strategies will be in limiting opportunism.

Where relational norms are weak or nonexistent, however, noncoercive strategies unfortunately may encourage opportunism. Indeed, the results suggest that, in the absence of strong relational norms, coercive influence techniques are more effective in limiting opportunism than noncoercive strategies are. Nevertheless, it is important to remember that coercive approaches must be considered as only short-term tactics, as they apparently provoke opportunism irrespective of the presence of relational norms.

Ultimately, the research added to a trend in the literature that finds that coercive influence strategies, applied under conditions of weak relational norms, provide, at best, only short-term relief from partner opportunism. Over the long run, however, coercive influence tends to exacerbate opportunistic behavior because it is seen as limiting a partner's autonomy. Opportunism is a common recourse in such cases. In the hospitality industry these outcomes may be even more likely, because a hotel manager and brand headquarters are more closely allied. If you enjoy good relations with your property managers, you will limit opportunism most effectively if you take the noncoercive approach.

---

1 Chekitan S. Dev, James R. Brown, and Dong Jin Lee, "Managing Marketing Relationships: Making Sure Everyone Plays on the Team," *Cornell Hotel and Restaurant Administration Quarterly* 41, no. 4 (2000): 10–20.

2 James R. Brown and Chekitan S. Dev, "The Franchisor-Franchisee Relationship: A Key To Franchise Performance," *Cornell Hotel and Restaurant Administration Quarterly* 38, no. 6 (1997): 30–38.

3 Jon Chavez, "After Doing the Math, Some Hotel Franchisees Consider Going Independent; Full Utilization of Travel Web Sites an Alternative to Brand Franchise Fees," *Blade,* May 30, 2004, http://www.hotel-online.com/News/PR2004_2nd/June04_Seagate.html (accessed January 31, 2012).

4 Innkeepers Trust, "Innkeepers USA Trust Acquires 182-Room Clarion Hotel in Downtown Louisville; Plans Repositioning to Hampton Inn Brand for All-In Cost of $60,000 per Key" (Innkeeper press release, Palm Beach, FL, June 28, 2004).

5 Kenneth H. Wathne and Jan B. Heide, "Opportunism in Interfirm Relationships: Forms, Outcomes, and Solutions," *Journal of Marketing* 64, no. 4 (2000): 36–51.

6 See, for example, Gary L. Frazier and Jagdish N. Sheth, "An Attitude-Behavior Framework for Distribution Channel Management," *Journal of Marketing* 49, no. 3 (1985): 38–48; Gary L. Frazier and John O. Summers, "Interfirm Influence Strategies and Their Application within Distribution Channels," *Journal of Marketing* 48, no. 3 (1984): 43–55; Gary L. Frazier and John O. Summers, "Perceptions of Interfirm Power and Its Use within a Franchise Channel of

Distribution," *Journal of Marketing Research* 23, no. 2 (1986): 169–76; Gary L. Frazier, James D. Gill, and Sudhir H. Kale, "Dealer Dependence Levels and Reciprocal Actions in a Channel of Distribution in a Developing Country," *Journal of Marketing* 53, no. 1 (1989): 50–69.

7 See, for example, Jakki Mohr and John. R. Nevin, "Communication Strategies in Marketing Channels: A Theoretical Perspective," *Journal of Marketing* 54, no. 4 (1990): 36–51; and Janice M. Payan and Richard G. McFarland, "Decomposing Influence Strategies: Argument Structure and Dependence as Determinants of the Effectiveness of Influence Strategies in Gaining Channel Member Compliance," *Journal of Marketing* 69, no. 3 (2005): 66–79.

8 See Dev, Brown, and Lee, "Managing Marketing Relationships"; Jan B. Heide and George John, "Do Norms Matter in Marketing Relationships?" *Journal of Marketing* 56, no. 2 (1992): 32–44; Patrick J. Kaufmann and Rajiv P. Dant, "The Dimensions of Commercial Exchange," *Marketing Letters* 3, no. 2 (1992): 171–85; Patrick J. Kaufmann and Louis W. Stern, "Relational Exchange Norms, Perceptions of Unfairness, and Retained Hostility in Commercial Litigation," *Journal of Conflict Resolution* 32, no. 3 (1988): 534–52; and Ian R. Macneil, *The New Social Contract* (New Haven, CT: Yale University Press, 1980).

9 Deepti Bhatnagar, "Evaluation of Managerial Influence Tactics: A Study of Indian Bank Managers," *Journal of Managerial Psychology* 8, no. 1 (1993): 3–9; Thomas T. Bonoma, "Conflict, Cooperation, and Trust in Three Power Systems," *Behavioral Science* 21, no. 6 (1976): 499–514; Jack J. Kasulis and Robert E. Spekman, "A Framework for the Use of Power," *European Journal of Marketing* 14, no. 4 (1980): 180–91; Cecilia M. Falbe and Gary Yukl, "Consequences for Managers of Using Single Influence Tactics and Combination of Tactics," *Academy of Management Journal* 35, no. 3 (1991): 638–52; Sandy D. Jap, Chris Manolis, and Barton A. Weitz, "Relationship Quality in Buyer-Seller Interactions in Channels of Distribution," *Journal of Business Research* 46, no. 3 (1999): 202–13; Jakki J. Mohr and Ravipreet S. Sohi, "Communication Flows in Distribution Channels: Impact on Assessments of Communication Quality and Satisfaction," *Journal of Retailing* 71, no. 4 (1995): 393–416; and Janice M. Payan and John R. Nevin, "Influence Strategy Efficacy in Supplier-Distributor Relationships," *Journal of Business Research* 59, no. 4 (2006): 457–65.

10 See Shankar S. Ganesan, "Determinants of Long-Term Orientation in Buyer-Seller Relationships," *Journal of Marketing* 58, no. 2 (1994): 1–19; Robert Lusch and James R. Brown, "A Modified Model of Power in the Marketing Channel," *Journal of Marketing Research* 19, no. 3 (1982): 312–23; Keith G. Provan and Steven J. Skinner, "Interorganizational Dependence and Control as Predictors of Opportunism in Dealer-Supplier Relations," *Academy of*

Management Journal 32, no. 1 (1989): 202–12; and Paul H. Schurr and Julie L. Ozanne, "Influences on Exchange Processes: Buyer's Preconceptions of a Seller's Trustworthiness and Bargaining Toughness," *Journal of Consumer Research* 11, no. 4 (1985): 939–53.

11 Brett Doyle, Robert Dwyer, Robert A. Robicheaux, and James T. Simpson, "Influence Strategies in Marketing Channels: Measures and Use in Different Relationship Structures," *Journal of Marketing Research* 29, no. 4 (1992): 462–73; Dev, Brown, and Lee, "Managing Marketing Relationships"; and Gary L. Frazier and Raymond C. Rody, "The Use of Influence Strategies in Interfirm Relationships in Industrial Product Channels," *Journal of Marketing* 55, no. 1 (1991): 52–69.

12 Richard M. Emerson, "Power-Dependence Relations," *American Sociological Review* 27, no. 1 (1962): 31–41; Frazier, Gill, and Kale, "Dealer Dependence Levels and Reciprocal Actions"; Ashwin W. Joshi, "How and Why Do Relatively Dependent Manufacturers Resist Supplier Power?" *Journal of Marketing Theory and Practice* 6, no. 4 (1998): 61–77; and Provan and Skinner, "Interorganizational Dependence and Control."

13 Frazier and Rody, "The Use of Influence Strategies"; Frazier and Summers, "Interfirm Influence Strategies"; James E. Stoddard, Janet E. Keith, and James R. Brown, "The Measurement of Influence Strategies in Distribution Channels: Scale Development and Testing," *Journal of Marketing Channels* 7, no. 4 (2000): 83–108.

CASE STUDY FOUR

Groupon

Ithaca-based Experience!The Finger Lakes (E!FL), which Laura Winter Falk had founded with her husband, Alan, was a tour operator offering guided tours and concierge services in the Finger Lakes region. After four years their venture was so successful that in 2010 the Falks had acquired a second touring van. However, demand in 2010 had begun to taper and they had not used their second van as often as they had hoped. The spring 2010 season had been particularly slow and the Falks were wondering how to increase growth and revenues. So far, they had relied on their website, referrals, and word of mouth to attract guests. Now, they were wondering whether they should adopt a more aggressive marketing strategy: signing up with Groupon, the online "social coupon" firm.[1]

In February 2011, the Falks contacted Groupon, which had just entered the Syracuse market not far from the Finger Lakes, to explore the possibility of having E!FL featured as a deal of the day. At first the Falks were pleasantly surprised when Groupon chose their proposal. But they found it difficult to craft a discounted tour that met the Groupon requirements, preserved E!FL's bottom line, and ensured continuing good relationships with their winery partners. Now, only a few weeks before the touring season, the Falks had to decide: should they or should they not Groupon?

An Overview of Groupon

Groupon's website features discounted gift certificates for local and national companies. It also sends offers to a list of subscribers to harness the collective buying power of its large user base by offering huge discounts on local services and products. While Groupon worked mostly with small retailers, it had also become famous for national deals, such as Gap Groupon, which went viral in August 2010, totaling $11 million.[2]

HISTORY

Groupon grew out of The Point Inc.,[3] a website platform for organizing all forms of collective social action, which was launched in November 2007 by Andrew Mason, current CEO of Groupon. The first market for Groupon was Chicago, where the company's headquarters were located, followed soon thereafter by Boston, New York City, Toronto, and eventually thirty cities. By March 2011, Groupon employed some fourteen hundred persons in the United States and four thousand overseas. The company had account executives in more than five hundred markets and regional offices in Europe, Latin America, and Asia.[4] The Groupon subscriber base had grown from 1.8 million in 2009 to 50 million in early 2011.[5]

BUSINESS MODEL

The company offered one Groupon deal per day to subscribers in each of the markets it served, making the deals visible on Facebook, Twitter, and Google. The deals were activated only when a minimum number of people agreed to buy (the "tip," in Groupon parlance), encouraging subscribers to share the promotion with family and friends. Once a deal tipped, the merchant and Groupon roughly split the revenue, and a group of customers had found themselves an unbeatable bargain. Groupon focused on customer care, accepting returns with no questions asked—even if a deal had been used—and maintaining a twenty-four-hour-a-day hotline.[6]

Groupon subscriber demographics were attractive. The typical Grouponer was young (68% were aged 18 to 34), was educated (50% had a bachelor's degree and 30% a graduate degree), was working (75% worked full time), was a single woman (77% were women and 49% were single), and had disposable income (48% earned over seventy thousand dollars a year).[7] Grouponers were habitual users of social media such as Facebook, Twitter, blogs, and YouTube.

To communicate to this audience, Groupon promoted its deals with a puckish, original writing style. Consequently, according to Groupon surveys, 66 percent of its subscribers read the Groupon write-ups every day. Apart from wanting deals, readers kept coming back to be entertained. The company employed seventy comedy writers who churned out the witty and whimsical pitches that accompanied the deals.[8]

Groupon coupons guaranteed merchants a minimum number of walk-in customers, no up-front cost to participate, and widespread exposure. Still, the company was selective, declining seven of every eight possible deals.[9] To be considered for a deal of the day, vendors needed outstanding reviews and substantial discount offers that would distinguish a Groupon deal from their other regular promotions. According to Groupon business surveys, 97 percent of firms using Groupon wanted to be featured again because Groupon had brought in quality customers (92% of respondents) who spent an average of 60 percent above the value of the Groupon and were likely to repeat (89% of respondents).

COMPETITORS

Although Groupon held a 60 percent market share in the social-couponing segment as of February 2010, it was not without competitors. With minimal barriers to entry, Groupon depended on its brand and first-mover advantage to maintain market share.[10] Only one competitor, LivingSocial, which had just received a $175 million investment from Amazon, was considered a serious competitor.[11] Together, Groupon and LivingSocial accounted for 92 percent of all web traffic in the social-couponing sector.[12]

Groupon also faced looming competition from Google and Facebook. In early 2011, reports surfaced that Google was planning to launch a competing product, called Google Offers, and Facebook began testing a social-buying program.[13] Indirect competition also came from the more traditional digital coupon companies such as coupons.com, the largest provider of digital coupons, with a value of $1 billion.[14] It received a $200 million private investment in 2011.[15]

To maintain its dominant position, Groupon increased its deal frequency to more than one per day in most markets and took on more small-business clients. It also started "Groupon Stores" in some markets to allow merchants to create their own deals. Since Groupon employees were not directly involved in these promotions, the firm accepted a cut of as low as 10 percent. The company was also investing in better data mining to personalize the deals based on variables such as gender, neighborhood, and buying history.

Finally, Groupon was extending its business into new market segments, such as travel. In June 2011, Mason announced "Groupon Getaways," a partnership with Expedia. The new venture would offer deep discounts on travel-related services by tapping into Expedia's access to 135,000 hotels, as well as car rental and cruise options.[16]

Working with Groupon

CRAFTING A GROUPON TOUR: EASIER SAID THAN DONE

Laura visited the Groupon website to learn more about the company and found it promising for E!FL's business:

> Groupon guaranteed walk-in customers from the Syracuse area, and we knew from our evaluation surveys that if we could get people in the door, they would probably come back and tour with us, especially if they came from close by. Also, their demographics made a good match for us; the majority of the fifty-five thousand registered Groupon users in the Syracuse market were primarily young, educated, female customers.

The Groupon ad would be optimal if the Groupon guests would occupy empty seats during the slow early spring season. For this to happen, the Falks had to move fast and have a coupon ad featured on Groupon by the end of March. In mid-January 2011, Laura submitted a request through the Groupon website. "The first contact was incredibly easy: I went on their website, watched a tutorial video, and filled in a three-question application form with the name of our company and a five-line description of its activity," Laura recalled.

Three weeks later, a Groupon representative covering the Syracuse area called the Falks to tell them that he was interested in running a Groupon coupon with E!FL. The conversation quickly turned into a brainstorming session on the type of tour E!FL could put together. Laura proposed a hotel package option, because she felt confident she could share the Groupon marketing cost with them, but the rep preferred to focus on the company's day tours, on the grounds that people coming from Syracuse would not want to stay in Ithaca, which was only about an hour away. Laura then proposed E!FL's two most popular tours as candidates for Groupon: Cayuga Wine Trail West Taste and Learn and Vinifera Varieties: Wines of the Seneca Lake Banana Belt.[17]

Laura announced that her goal was to attract at least one hundred new customers through a Groupon ad. Based on previous Groupon wine-tasting promotions in the Syracuse area, the rep estimated that E!FL would get a minimum of seventy-five buyers. In November 2010, a Groupon promotion sold 261 coupons for a five-dollar wine tasting and bottle of wine, a fifteen-dollar value at Syracuse's Lakeland Winery, which is in the business of providing varietal juices to would-be winemakers. Another Groupon, in January 2011, offered a wine tasting and pairing for two, plus a wine card from the Finger Lakes wine trail wineries. Valued at seventy dollars, this thirty-dollar offer generated fifty-one purchases. "The fewer restrictions you put on the Groupon, the better it will sell," the rep insisted, alluding to limits on the duration of promotion and redemption of coupons, upper limits on the number of coupons to be sold, or limits on the number of coupons per person. The discussion then moved to pricing:

> According to [the rep], we had to propose at least a 50 percent discount [a tour at forty-five dollars per person] to make the coupon attractive. I pointed out that since Groupon would take half, I would in fact sell my tour at a 75 percent discount, which would result in our losing money with each sale.

Next, the rep offered advice on how E!FL could mitigate costs while preserving the attractiveness of the ad:

> His recommendation was to keep the 50 percent discount but to raise the value of the tour to $110 [a fifty-five-dollar coupon], for example by adding a free twenty-dollar bottle of wine or some twenty dollars worth of coupons on wine purchases. This meant that the wineries would have to agree to share with E!FL the cost of the Groupon ad campaign, and it was likely that only a few would buy in.

Laura asked the rep for a couple of days to contact the wineries and see whether the deal was feasible. First, she called one of E!FL's largest winery partners. The winery was receptive, but it advised against the free bottle of wine, pointing out that it would put wineries in a delicate situation vis-à-vis their distributors. Meanwhile, Laura carefully estimated the maximum cost she could afford per Groupon guest versus a regular paying guest for E!FL to break even. That is, she needed to calculate the sustainable cost for a tour for, say, six guests, if all of them used a Groupon. She reached the following conclusion:

> Increased value was a good idea, but it was clear that we also needed to decrease our costs, such as the wine-tasting fees, which represented the largest chunk of our costs. If they could be waived, we would cover our

cost for each Groupon guest with the minimum of six guests per tour. But I needed a fast answer from the wineries so the Groupon ad could be posted on the web by the end of March.

Laura e-mailed all her winery partners, inviting them to join the Groupon deal. She underlined its benefits in terms of brand exposure (fifty-five thousand viewers for one day and an estimate of seventy-five to one hundred walk-in customers) and asked them to share some of the cost by waiving tasting fees and to increase value by offering some sort of discount on purchased items. Within two days, four Seneca Lake wineries agreed to waive their fees and offer a five-dollar discount on wine purchases. Laura proposed the following E!FL tour coupon to Groupon: a fifty-five-dollar guided wine tour of the Seneca Lake Banana Belt that included visits to four wineries with a free tasting at each and a five-dollar discount on a wine purchase (up to $110 in value). The following day, Groupon accepted that proposal and e-mailed the Falks a contract.

NEGOTIATING THE CONTRACT

Although the two parties had worked out the deal's outlines, the devil is always in the details. In addition to the proposed tour coupon, the rough draft of the Groupon contract contained the company's merchant account terms and conditions. Examining these details, Alan determined that many contractual aspects still needed to be negotiated. "I was not as enthusiastic as Laura because in my opinion the contract protected more the interests of Groupon than ours; Groupon's interest was to sell as many coupons as possible; ours was to gain a manageable number of discount guests who would spread the buzz and bring additional business."

As a marketing company, Groupon's responsibility ended when the customers bought the coupons online. It was not liable for operational factors such as number of coupons sold, when coupon holders would choose to redeem their coupons, or whether coupon buyers would be onetime-only visitors, existing customers, or purchasers of multiple coupons. Alan noted both the reports of small businesses that enjoyed huge sales days and an influx of new customers thanks to Groupon and cautionary tales about disappointed small businesses that ended up losing money because they saw too few customers, too many customers, or the wrong kind of customers. An independent academic research study found significantly lower satisfaction levels with Groupon business deals than with those advertised by Groupon on its website.[18] Out of 150 Groupon businesses interviewed for the study, 32 percent said they made no money from them, and 42 percent said that they would not do another daily deal. Disappointed retailers cited a low rate of repeat Groupon customers buying at full price and a low rate of Groupon customer spending beyond the coupon value. The study also referred to previous research showing that price discounts eroded brand value in the long term.

Consequently, the Falks set up a list of the contractual terms they wanted to discuss:

Multiple-coupon-buying customers: To gain the maximum number of new visitors, the Falks wanted to limit coupon sales to one per person (nontransferable), with two additional ones as gifts.

Length of redemption period: The Falks had no way of controlling exactly when Groupon guests would redeem their coupons. They had limited control over when their ad would go online, since Groupon's policy was to not commit to a specific date to feature the ad.[19] They wanted the ad to specify that an online reservation was required for the coupon and that space was subject to availability. Requiring reservations had two functions. In addition to the obvious one of setting up tours, this would also give them access to the names and e-mails of the prospective Groupon guests. Once the tour was reserved, the buyer would present the Groupon voucher before the tour, showing the Groupon number and the name of the main buyer. Since they ran a seasonal business, the Falks did not want to extend the offer into the next season. They knew the coupon would have an expiration date, but were not sure about the ideal redemption deadline.

Coupon cap: Alan was also concerned about the possibility of being overwhelmed by Groupon customers as well as lost revenue. "No upfront cost did not mean the Groupon was free, even if we covered our costs with the Seneca tour .... We needed to structure our deal further by restricting the number of coupons sold, as E!FL and our partners could not handle an onslaught of Groupon guests." E!FL would not lose money on Groupon guests, but it would have to forgo $62.50 in revenue.[20] At five hundred coupons sold, for instance, the forgone revenue would be $15,248, or the equivalent of 284 repeat or new guests paying full fare. But Laura was reluctant to cap the deal, for fear of making the coupon unattractive to Groupon: "We are a little fish; they do not need us."

Credit card processing fee: Most contracts with Groupon passed the 2.5-percent credit card transaction fees on to the merchant. Groupon collected customer payment, distributed Groupon vouchers, and mailed merchants checks for net proceeds. Since E!FL would receive only half of a coupon's value, Alan wanted Groupon at least to cut the credit card fee in half, if not waive it entirely.

The Groupon "editorial" or ad: To maintain its web persona, Groupon required merchants to relinquish their right to write or coedit their ad, except for including specific facts. Groupon took care of the copy to ensure that every Groupon ad was "engaging, entertaining, and non-intrusive" and resonated with their subscribers. The Falks were worried that, to entertain its subscribers, Groupon would downplay the educational and cultural aspects of an E!FL tour and focus instead on drinking, thereby attracting the wrong kind of guests. While numerous wineries cater to guests who seek entertainment, the four wineries on this tour directed their attention to educating guests about their wines and production methods. Besides, to honor their engagement, the Falks had to have the name of the four Seneca wineries on the tour shown high up on the advertisement.

Should They Take the Leap of Faith?

This last issue embodied the Falks' biggest concern. There was no way to negotiate a contract that ensured that they would not attract the wrong kind of guests: people who were interested in overdrinking and who would spoil the experience for other guests. They were also concerned about the onetime bargain hunters who would not use the five-dollar voucher to buy a bottle of wine and who would not tip the guides; or the existing E!FL customer who, after using a Groupon, would not buy the tour at full fare again. Worst would be a guest with unrealistic expectations: "One bad review on Trip Advisor can go a long way," remarked Alan. As Groupon explained on its website, "Our subscribers are not looking for 'the perfect deal,' they're looking for the perfect excuse to try something new; we get them to your business, and you bring them back again and again."

---

1 Christopher Steiner, "The Next Web Phenom," *Forbes,* August 30, 2010, 58–62.

2 Wailing Woong, "Gap's Groupon Pulls in $11 Million," *Chicago Tribune,* August 20, 2010. The Gap Groupon was a twenty-five-dollar coupon for fifty

dollars worth of merchandise. http://articles.chicagotribune.com/2010-08-20/business/sc-biz-0821-groupon-20100820_1_gender-and-zip-code-chicago-startup-coupon-site (accessed June 1, 2011).

3 The Point was privately owned and backed by individual private investors, New Enterprise Associates (a venture capital firm that helped grow CareerBuilder, Vonage, and UUNET), Accel Partners (a venture capital firm that invested in Facebook, Etsy, comScore, and StumbleUpon), and Digital Sky Technologies (an Internet investment firm that invested in Facebook and Zynga).

4 Groupon, http://www.groupon.com/about (accessed June, 5, 2011).

5 Jennifer Saba and Clare Baldwin, "Groupon Worth $25 Billion? Nope," Reuters, March 15, 2011.

6 Bari Weiss, "Groupon's $6 Billion Gambler," *Wall Street Journal,* December 18, 2010, http://online.wsj.com/article/SB10001424052748704828104576021481410635432.html (accessed June 1, 2011).

7 Groupon, http://www.grouponworks.com/why-groupon/comparison-guide (accessed June 5, 2011).

8 For example, consider the following copy for a Groupon for microderm-abrasion treatment at a spa: "Removing the top layer of skin from a face is good for more than just solving every single Scooby-Doo mystery; it can also result in a smoother, healthier face." Groupon, "Spa Space—West Loop," http://www.groupon.com/deals/spa-space (accessed February 1, 2012).

9 Weiss, "Groupon's $6 Billion Gambler."

10 neXtup Research, "Groupon Anxiety," *Economist,* March 19, 2011, http://www.economist.com/node/18388904 (accessed June 1, 2012).

11 Bill Saporito, "The Groupon Clipper," *Time,* February 21, 2011, http://www.time.com/time/magazine/article/0,9171,2048311,00.html (accessed February 1, 2012).

12 According to December site-visit data compiled by Experian Hitwise, a research and analysis firm. Annie Lowrey, "Group Coupon Sites: Boom Business or Bubble?" *Washington Post,* January 16, 2011, http://www.washingtonpost.com/wp-dyn/content/article/2011/01/15/AR2011011500297.html (accessed June 1, 2011)

13 Saporito, "The Groupon Clipper."

14 Evelyn M. Rusli, "With Eye on Public Offering, Coupons.com Attracts Big Investments," *New York Times,* June 9, 2011, http://dealbook.nytimes.com/2011/06/09/coupons-com-raises-200-million/ (accessed June 1, 2011).

15 Founded in 1998, Coupons.com survived the dot-com boom and bust, allowing users to download and print coupons from traditional purveyors such as Clorox, General Mills, Kmart, and Walgreens. Its network spanned thousands of sites, including those of retailers, publishers, consumer electronics, shopping cards, and apps.

16 Geoffrey A. Fowler, "Groupon Launches Deal Site with Expedia," *Wall Street Journal,* June 1, 2011, http://online.wsj.com/article/SB100014240527023037453045 76359911541840704.html (accessed June 5, 2011)

17 The region around Seneca Lake had become known as the "Banana Belt," because of its extraordinary microclimate, which was ideal for growing European vinifera grapes.

18 Utpal M. Dholakia, "How Effective Are Groupon Promotions for Businesses?" (September 28, 2010), http://ssrn.com/abstract=1696327 or http://dx.doi.org/10.2139/ssrn.1696327 (accessed June 1, 2011)

19 "Groupon reserves the right to feature anything in our pipeline at any time, just in case there are time-sensitive deals that come to our attention at the last minute. We use metrics and past trends to determine the best placement for each feature. To make sure you have time to prepare your business and that all questions have been answered, we always contact you before we feature your business," http://www.grouponworks.com/faqs (accessed June 1, 2011).

20 By comparison, if E!FL had created the same 50 percent–off sale and promoted it via Facebook Ads instead, for $63.88 forgone revenue per guest, at $0.5 per click, the ad would have generated $63.88/0.5 = 127.76 chances to make a sale, that is, a conversion rate from click to sale of $(1/127.76 \times 100) = 0.78\%$. Hence, to outperform Groupon, a minimum conversion rate goal of 0.78 percent would need to be achieved.

Acknowledgments

This book harvests the fruits of more than twenty years of scholarly work as well as many years of education and training that prepared me for what has been a most rewarding life immersed in the theory and practice of hospitality marketing and branding. I would not have been able to write it without the support and assistance of many people, whose contributions I deeply appreciate.

My professional hospitality initiation benefited immensely from the inspiration of many industry leaders, including Rai Bahadur M. S. Oberoi, Mr. P. R. S. Oberoi, Mr. Alan Fernandes, Ms. Ragini Chopra, and Mr. BVSAN Murthy. In graduate school, I was fortunate to be tutored by wonderful teachers and scholars, among them Dean Bob Beck, Paul Beals, Gerard Guibilato, Mike Rimmington, Robert Lewis, Kent Monroe, and Jim Brown. I thank them all for providing me with a strong foundation and for their ongoing encouragement as my academic career progressed. Each has inspired me uniquely.

I thank my PhD committee chair, Michael Olsen, for the unstinting personal and professional support he provided as I embarked on my scholarly journey. Mike and his family—Sandy, Mike Jr., and Kelly—saw me through the ups and downs of academic life and never failed to boost my spirits when they needed boosting. I am grateful for Mike's encouragement, advice, and friendship.

I owe a special debt of gratitude to my coauthors, who generously shared their passion and expertise as we worked together on the research that informs most of the chapters in this book. Their collaboration enriched my work at every step and improved the conceptual clarity and scholarly rigor of these projects. They are, in alphabetical order: Sanjeev Agarwal, Eric Anderson, John Bowen, Jim Brown, John Buschman, Krishna Erramilli, Laura Falk, Stephen Grzeskowiak, Weizhong Jiang, Dong-Jin Lee, Mike Morgan, Gabe Piccoli, Kesh Prasad, Vithala Rao, Aveek Sengupta, Stowe Shoemaker, Laure Stroock,

John Thomas, Glenn Withiam, and Kevin Zhou. I look forward to future collaborations with these and other scholars as I continue to track and analyze trends in hospitality marketing and branding.

My many colleagues at Cornell University's School of Hotel Administration, Harvard Business School, the University of Buckingham, Florida International University, the University of Denver, and at many academic and industry conferences and seminars where I have had the pleasure and honor of presenting my work provided valuable collaborative and critical feedback and support over the years, in both formal and informal discussions.

In my more than three decade–long association with the hospitality industry, and more than two decades of service on the faculty of Cornell's Hotel School, I have had the pleasure and privilege of befriending many hospitality leaders who have encouraged me to challenge conventional wisdom and have supported my work. A special thanks to Ajay Bakaya, Scott Berman, Bill Callnin, David Corsun, Fred DeMicco, Satinder Dhillon, Bob Gilbert, Al Gomes, Leo Hart, Rajiv Kaul, J. T. Kuhlman, Mike Leven, John Longstreet, James McBride, Sid Narang, Vikram Oberoi, Priya Paul, Mike Pusateri, Lulu Raghavan, H. P. Rama, Jim Renard, Stephan Riegel, Tom Seddon, Arjun Singh, Ramesh Srinivasan, Sanjiv Suri, Joe West, Scott Wiggins, Mark Woodworth, and Peter Yesawich. These relationships have helped shape the contours of my approach to marketing and branding studies and for that I am very grateful indeed.

I thank my over ten thousand students now spread all over the world for suffering through the initial formulations of these projects and offering their insights and responses to the key findings. By sharing with me at least some of the growing pains of scholarly work, they have provided a fresh perspective that would otherwise be unavailable.

I am very grateful to Peter Potter, editor in chief at Cornell University Press, for his steadfast support and invaluable guidance in the development of this project. Peter's counsel has made the process immeasurably easier to navigate.

I thank my personal editor, Bill Barnett, for, among other things, helping me distill the most important insights from my work, making it accessible to a wider audience.

Ultimately, my career has depended on and thrived in the warm light of the love and inspiration of my family. Heartfelt gratitude goes out to my mother, Kamal, my father, Yashpal, and my sisters, Poonam and Anjana, for giving me a loving and caring foundation on which to build my life and work. I thank my beautiful and talented wife, Joyce, and my two wonderful sons, Andrew and

Christopher, who have persevered through countless nights, weekends, and holidays devoted to working on the papers that form the basis of this book. They have never wavered in their love and support of my professional endeavors and it is for their love and support that I am forever thankful. Without my family I would never have realized my personal and professional dreams.

The chapters of this book are adaptations and updates of previously published articles.

Chapter 1: Chekitan S. Dev, John D. Buschman, and John T. Bowen, "Hospitality Marketing: A Retrospective Analysis (1960–2010) and Predictions (2010–2020)," *Cornell Hospitality Quarterly* 51, no. 4 (2010): 459–69.

Chapter 2: Chekitan S. Dev and Glenn Withiam, "Fresh Thinking about the Box," *Cornell Center for Hospitality Research Brand Roundtable Proceedings,* 3, no. 6 (June 2011).

Chapter 3: Gabriele Piccoli and Chekitan S. Dev. "Emerging Marketing Channels in Hospitality: A Global Study of Internet-Enabled Flash Sales and Private Sales," *Cornell Center for Hospitality Research Report* 12, no. 15 (February 2012).

Chapter 4: Chekitan S. Dev, "Carnival Cruise Lines: Charting A New Brand Course," *Cornell Hospitality Quarterly* 47 no. 3 (2006): 1–8.

Chapter 5: Chekitan S. Dev, James R. Brown, and Kevin Zheng Zhou, "Global Brand Expansion: How to Select a Market Entry Strategy," *Cornell Hospitality Quarterly* 48, no. 1 (2007): 13–27.

Chapter 6: Chekitan S. Dev, M. Krishna Erramilli, and Sanjeev Agarwal. "Brands across Borders: Choosing between Franchising and Management Contracts for Entering International Markets," *Cornell Hospitality Quarterly* 43, no. 6 (2002): 91–104.

Chapter 7: Chekitan S. Dev, Kevin Zheng Zhou, James R. Brown, and Sanjeev Agarwal, "Customer Orientation or Competitor Orientation: Which Marketing Strategy Has a Higher Payoff for Hotel Brands?," *Cornell Hospitality Quarterly* 50, no. 1 (2009): 19–28.

Chapter 8: Chekitan S. Dev, John H. Thomas, John Buschman, and Eric Anderson, "Brand Rights and Hotel Management Agreements: Lessons from Ritz-Carlton Bali's Lawsuit against The Ritz-Carlton Hotel Company," *Cornell Hospitality Quarterly* 51, no. 2 (2010): 215–30.

Chapter 9: Keshav Prasad and Chekitan S. Dev, "Managing Hotel Brand Equity: A Customer-centric Framework for Assessing Performance," *Cornell Hotel and Restaurant Administration Quarterly* 41, no. 3 (2000): 22–31.

Chapter 10: Chekitan S. Dev, Michael Morgan, and Stowe Shoemaker. "A Positioning Analysis of Hotel Brands Based on Travel Manager Perceptions," *Cornell Hotel and Restaurant Administration Quarterly* 36, no. 6 (1995): 48–55.

Chapter 11: Weizhong Jiang, Chekitan S. Dev, and Vithala R. Rao. "Brand Extension and Customer Loyalty: Evidence from the Lodging Industry," *Cornell Hotel and Restaurant Administration Quarterly* 43, no. 4 (2002): 5–16.

Chapter 12: Aveek Sengupta and Chekitan S. Dev, "Service Innovation: Applying the 7-I Model to Improve Brand Positioning at the Taj Holiday Village Goa, India," *Cornell Hospitality Quarterly* 52, no. 1 (2011): 11–19.

Chapter 13: Chekitan S. Dev, James R. Brown, and Dong-Jin Lee, "Managing Marketing Relationships: Making Sure Everyone Plays on the Team," *Cornell Hotel and Restaurant Administration Quarterly* 41, no. 4 (2000): 10–20.

Chapter 14: James R. Brown and Chekitan S. Dev, "The Franchisor-Franchisee Relationship: A Key to Franchise Performance," *Cornell Hotel and Restaurant Administration Quarterly* 38, no. 6 (1997): 30–38.

Chapter 15: Chekitan S. Dev, Stephan Grzeskowiak, and James R. Brown, "Opportunism in Brand Partnerships: Effects of Coercion and Relational Norms," *Cornell Hospitality Quarterly* 53, no. 4 (2011): 377–87.

Chapter 16: Chekitan S. Dev, Laura Winter Falk, and Laure Mougeot Stroock, "To Groupon or Not to Groupon: A Tour Operator's Dilemma," *Cornell Center for Hospitality Research Report* 11, no. 19 (November 2011).

Bibliography

Aaker, David. *Building Strong Brands.* New York: Free Press, 1996.

——. *Managing Brand Equity.* New York: Free Press, 1991.

Aaker, David, and Kevin Keller. "Consumer Evaluations of Brand Extensions." *Journal of Marketing* 54, no. 1 (1990): 27–41.

Anderson, Erin, and Hubert Gatignon. "Modes of Foreign Entry: A Transaction Cost Analysis and Propositions." *Journal of International Business Studies* 17, no. 3 (1986): 1–26.

Anderson, Erin, and Barton A. Weitz. "Make-or-Buy Decisions: Vertical Integration and Marketing Productivity." *Sloan Management Review* 27, no. 3 (1986): 3–19.

Arndt, Johan. "Toward a Concept of Domesticated Markets." *Journal of Marketing* 43, no. 4 (1979): 69–75.

Arnold, David. *The Handbook of Brand Management.* Boston: Addison-Wesley, 1992.

Arora, Ashish, and Andrea Fosfuri. "Wholly Owned Subsidiary versus Technology Licensing in the Worldwide Chemical Industry." *Journal of International Business Studies* 3, no. 4 (2000): 555–72.

Baloglu, Seymus. "Dimensions of Customer Loyalty: Separating Friends from Well Wishers." *Cornell Hospitality and Restaurant Administration Quarterly* 43, no. 1 (2002): 47–59.

Barney, Jay. "Firm Resources and Sustained Competitive Advantage." *Journal of Management* 17, no. 1 (1991): 99–120.

Barsky, Jonathan, and Leonard Nash. "Evoking Emotion: Affective Keys to Hotel Loyalty." *Cornell Hotel and Restaurant Administration Quarterly* 43, no. 1 (2002): 39–46.

Bello, Daniel C., and David I. Gilliland, "The Effect of Output Controls, Process Controls, and Flexibility on Export Channel Performance." *Journal of Marketing* 61, no. 1 (1997): 22–38.

Bhatnagar, Deepti. "Evaluation of Managerial Influence Tactics: A Study of Indian Bank Managers." *Journal of Managerial Psychology* 8, no. 1 (1993): 3–9.

Bliss, Robert L. "PLAN Your Public Relations Program: A Public Relations Counsel Outlines a Program of Successful Community Service for Hotel Men." *Cornell Hotel and Restaurant Administration Quarterly* 1, no. 3 (1960): 29–31.

Bonoma, Thomas T. "Conflict, Cooperation, and Trust in Three Power Systems." *Behavioral Science* 21, no. 6 (1976): 499–514.

Bowen, John T., and Stowe Shoemaker. "Loyalty: A Strategic Commitment." *Cornell Hospitality and Restaurant Administration Quarterly* 39, no. 1 (1998): 12–23.

Boyle, Brett, F. Robert Dwyer, Robert A. Robicheaux, and James T. Simpson. "Influence Strategies in Marketing Channels: Measures and Use in Different Relationship Structures." *Journal of Marketing Research* 29, no. 4 (1992): 462–73.

Brown, James R., and Chekitan S. Dev. "The Franchisor-Franchisee Relationship: A Key to Franchise Performance." *Cornell Hotel and Restaurant Administration Quarterly* 38, no. 6 (1997): 30–38.

Bursk, Edward C. "The Marketing Concept: A New Approach to Hotel Management: Alert Hosts in the Marketing Age." *Cornell Hotel and Restaurant Administration Quarterly* 7, no. 4 (1967): 2–8.

Campbell-Smith, Graham. "Marketing the Meal Experience." *Cornell Hotel and Restaurant Administration Quarterly* 11, no. 1 (1970): 73–102.

Chandler, Gaylen N., and Steven H. Hanks. "Market Attractiveness, Resource-Based Capabilities, Venture Strategies, and Venture Performance." *Journal of Business Venturing* 9, no. 4 (1994): 331–49.

Chavez, Jon. "After Doing the Math, Some Hotel Franchisees Consider Going Independent; Full Utilization of Travel Web Sites an Alternative to Brand Franchise Fees." *Blade,* May 30, 2004. http://www.hotel-online.com/News/PR2004_2nd/June04_Seagate.html (accessed January 31, 2012).

Choi, C. J., and Carlo Scarpa. "Credible Spatial Preemption through Reputation Extension," *International Journal of Industrial Organization* 10, no. 3 (1992): 439–47.

Choi, Sunmee, and Sheryl Kimes. "Electronic Distribution Channels' Effect on Hotel Revenue Management." *Cornell Hotel and Restaurant Administration Quarterly* 43, no. 3 (2002): 23–31.

Coffman, C. Dewitt. *Marketing for a Full House.* Ithaca, NY: Cornell Hotel and Restaurant Administration Quarterly, 1972.

Collis, David J., and Cynthia A. Montgomery. "Competing on Resources: Strategy in the 1990s." *Harvard Business Review* 73, no. 4 (1995): 118–28.

Conner, Kathleen R., and C. K. Prahalad. "A Resource-based Theory of the Firm: Knowledge versus Opportunism." *Organization Science* 7, no. 5 (1996): 477–501.

Contractor, Farok J., and Sumit K. Kundu. "Franchising versus Company-Run Operations: Modal Choice in the Global Hotel Sector." *Journal of International Marketing* 6, no. 2 (1998): 28–53.

——. "Modal Choice in a World of Alliances: Analyzing Organizational Forms in the International Hotel Sector." *Journal of International Business Studies* 29, no. 2 (1998): 325–58.

Cornell Hotel and Restaurant Administration Quarterly. "Reservation Systems: Communication Network That Sells the Rooms." *Cornell Hotel and Restaurant Administration Quarterly* 8, no. 4 (1968): 11–16.

Crandell, Chad, Kristie Dickinson, and Fern Kanter. "Negotiating the Hotel Management Contract." In *Hotel Asset Management: Principles and Practices*, ed. Paul Beals and Greg Denton, 85–104. Lansing, MI: Educational Institute of the American Hotel Motel and Lodging Association, 2003.

"Daily Deal Trends in North America." *Yipit Data Report*, August 12, 2011. http://www.digitaltrends.com/web/despite-downward-trend-groupon-revenue-grew-13-percent-in-august/ (accessed September 26, 2011).

Dant, Rajiv P., and Patrick L. Schul. "Conflict Resolution Processes in Contractual Channels of Distribution." *Journal of Marketing* 56, no. 1 (1992): 43.

Davison, Mark L. *Multidimensional Scaling*. New York: John Wiley and Sons, 1983.

Day, George S., and P. Nedungadi. "Managerial Representations of Competitive Advantage." *Journal of Marketing* 58, no. 2 (1994): 31–44.

Day, George S., and Robin Wensley. "Assessing Advantage," *Journal of Marketing* 52, no. 2 (1988): 1–20.

Dev, Chekitan S., Expert Report. "Rebuttals to the Critiques of My Opinions by: Dr. Jeffery Alan Durbin and Mr. Roger Cline." In Civil Action No 8:05-cv-00787-PJM, *P. T. Karang Mas Sejahtera,* Plaintiff, *v. Marriott International, Inc.,* et al., Defendants.

Dev, Chekitan S., and Ellis D. Bernard. "Guest Histories: An Untapped Service Resource." *Cornell Hospitality and Restaurant Administration Quarterly* 32, no. 2 (1991): 28.

Dev, Chekitan S., and James R. Brown. "Franchising and Other Operating Arrangements in the Lodging Industry: A Strategic Comparison." *Journal of Hospitality and Tourism Research* 14, no. 3 (1991): 25.

———. "Marketing Strategy, Vertical Structure, and Performance in the Lodging Industry: A Contingency Approach." *International Journal of Hospitality Management* 9, no. 3 (1990): 269–82.

Dev, Chekitan S., James R. Brown, and Dong Jin Lee. "Managing Marketing Relationships: Making Sure Everyone Plays on the Team." *Cornell Hotel and Restaurant Administration Quarterly* 41, no. 4 (2000): 10–20.

Dev, Chekitan S., M. Krishna Erramilli, and Sanjeev Agarwal. "Brands across Borders: Choosing between Franchising and Management Contracts for Entering International Markets." *Cornell Hotel and Restaurant Administration Quarterly* 43, no. 6 (2002): 91–104.

Dev, Chekitan S., Michael Morgan, and Stowe Shoemaker. "A Positioning Analysis of Hotel Brands." *Cornell Hotel and Restaurant Administration Quarterly* 36, no. 6 (1995): 48–55.

Dholakia, Utpal M. "How Effective Are Groupon Promotions for Businesses?" Rice University–Jesse H. Jones Graduate School of Management (September 28, 2010).

Dorf, David C. "Package Plan Promotion." *Cornell Hotel and Restaurant Administration Quarterly* 2, no. 3 (1961): 51–54.

Doyle, Brett, Robert Dwyer, Robert A. Robicheaux, and James T. Simpson, "Influence Strategies in Marketing Channels: Measures and Use in Different Relationship Structures." *Journal of Marketing Research* 29, no. 4 (1992): 462–73.

Dubé, Laurette, and Leo M. Renaghan. "Building Customer Loyalty: Guests'
Perspectives on the Lodging Industry's Functional Best Practices." *Cornell
Hospitality and Restaurant Administration Quarterly* 40, no. 5 (1999): 78–88.

Dubé, Laurette, Leo M. Renaghan, and Jane M. Miller. "Measuring Customer
Satisfaction for Strategic Management." *Cornell Hospitality and Restaurant
Administration Quarterly* 35, no. 1 (1994): 39–47.

Dunning, John H. *Explaining International Production.* London: Unwin Hyman,
1988, 242–65.

Dwyer, F. Robert, Paul F. Schurr, and Sejo Oh. "Developing Buyer-Seller Relationships." *Journal of Marketing* 51, no. 2 (1987): 11–27.

Ekeledo, Iketchi, and K. Sivakumar. "Foreign Market Entry Mode Choice of
Service Firms: A Contingency Perspective." *Journal of the Academy of
Marketing Science* 26, no. 4 (1998): 274–92.

Emerson, Richard M. "Power-Dependence Relations." *American Sociological Review*
27, no. 1 (1962): 31–41.

Erramilli, M. Krishna, Sanjeev Agarwal, and Chekitan. S. Dev. "Choice between
Non-equity Entry Modes: An Organizational Capability Perspective."
Journal of International Business Studies 33, no. 2 (2002): 223–42.

Fahy, John, Graham Hooley, Tony Cox, Jozsef Beracs, Krzysztof Fonfara, and Boris
Snoj. "The Development and Impact of Marketing Capabilities in Central
Europe." *Journal of International Business Studies* 31, no. 1 (2000): 63–81.

Falbe, Cecilia M., and Gary Yukl. "Consequences for Managers of Using Single
Influence Tactics and Combination of Tactics." *Academy of Management
Journal* 35, no. 3 (1991): 638–52.

Farquhar, Peter H., Julia A. Han, Paul M. Herr, and Yuji Ijiri, "Strategies for
Leveraging Master Brands: How to Bypass the Risks of Direct Extensions."
Marketing Research 4, no. 3 (1992): 32–43.

Fowler, Geoffrey A. "Groupon Launches Deal Site With Expedia." *Wall Street
Journal,* June 1, 2011.

Frazier, Gary L., and Raymond C. Rody. "The Use of Influence Strategies in Interfirm Relationships in Industrial Product Channels." *Journal of Marketing* 55,
no. 1 (1991): 52–69.

Frazier, Gary L., and Jagdish N. Sheth. "An Attitude-Behavior Framework for
Distribution Channel Management." *Journal of Marketing* 49, no. 3
(1985): 38–48.

Frazier, Gary L., and John O. Summers. "Interfirm Influence Strategies and their
Application within Distribution Channels." *Journal of Marketing* 48, no. 3
(1984): 43–55.

——. "Perceptions of Interfirm Power and Its Use within a Franchise Channel of
Distribution." *Journal of Marketing Research* 23, no. 2 (1986): 169–76.

Frazier, Gary L., James D. Gill, and Sudhir H. Kale. "Dealer Dependence Levels
and Reciprocal Actions in a Channel of Distribution in a Developing Country." *Journal of Marketing* 53, no. 1 (1989): 50–69.

Frey, Bruno S. "Does Monitoring Increase Work Effort? The Rivalry with Trust and
Loyalty." *Economic Inquiry* 31, no. 4 (1993): 663–70.

Fulgoni, Gian [executive chairman and cofounder, comScore Inc.]. "Monetizing the Internet through Sales and Advertising." PowerPoint presentation, Chicago Digital Collective Summit, Chicago, April 2011.

Gabszewicz, Jean, Lynne Pepall, and Jacques-Francois Thisse. "Sequential Entry with Brand Loyalty Caused by Consumer Learning-by-Using." *Journal of Industrial Economics* 40, no. 4 (1992): 397–416.

Galb, Jim. "Taking off the Gloves." *ASTA Agency Management* 66, no. 8 (1993): 95.

Ganesan, Shankar S. "Determinants of Long-Term Orientation in Buyer-Seller Relationships." *Journal of Marketing* 58, no. 2 (1994): 1–19.

Gassenheimer, Jule B., David B. Baucus, and Melissa S. Baucus. "Cooperative Arrangements among Entrepreneurs: An Analysis of Opportunism and Communication in Franchise Structures." *Journal of Business Research* 36, no. 1 (1996): 67–79.

Gatignon, Hubert, and Erin Anderson. "The Multinational Corporations' Degree of Control over Foreign Subsidiaries: An Empirical Test of a Transaction Cost Explanation." *Journal of Law, Economics, and Organization* 4, no. 2 (1988) 305–36.

Gilbert, Richard J., and Carmen Matutes. "Product-Line Rivalry with Brand Differentiation." *Journal of Industrial Economics* 41, no. 3 (1993): 223–40.

Goldberg, Victor P. "Relational Exchange: Economics and Complex Contracts." *American Behavioral Scientist* 23, no. 3 (1980): 337–52.

Grabowski, Henry G., and John M. Vernon. "Brand Loyalty, Entry, and Price Competition in Pharmaceuticals after the 1984 Drug Act." *Journal of Law and Economics* 35, no. 2 (1992): 331–50.

Grohman, H. Victor. "Internal Promotion for Hotels." *Cornell Hotel and Restaurant Administration Quarterly* 2, no. 3 (1961): 29–35.

Hardy, Kenneth G., and Alan J. Magrath, "Dealing with Cheating in Distribution." *European Journal of Marketing* 23, no. 2 (1989): 123.

Harris, Mark. "Economical Positioning." *Cornell Hotel and Restaurant Administration Quarterly* 29, no. 2 (1988): 97.

Heide, Jan B. "Interorganizational Governance in Marketing Channels." *Journal of Marketing* 58, no. 1 (1994): 71–85.

Heide, Jan B., and George John. "Alliances in Industrial Purchasing: The Determinants of Joint Action in Buyer-Supplier Relationships." *Journal of Marketing Research* 27, no. 1 (1990): 24–36.

———. "Do Norms Matter in Marketing Relationships?" *Journal of Marketing* 56, no. 2 (1992): 32–44.

Hu, Yao-Su. "The International Transferability of the Firm's Advantages." *California Management Review* 37, no. 4 (1995): 73–88.

Hwang, Peter, and W. Chan Kim. "An Eclectic Theory of the Choice of International Entry Mode." *Strategic Management Journal* 11, no. 2 (1990): 117–28.

Innkeepers Trust. "Innkeepers USA Trust Acquires 182-Room Clarion Hotel in Downtown Louisville; Plans Repositioning to Hampton Inn Brand for All-In Cost of $60,000 Per Key." Innkeeper press release, Palm Beach, FL June 28, 2004.

Ireland, Norman J. *Product Differentiation and Quality: The New Industrial Economics.* Ed. G. Norman and M. La Manna. Brookfield, VT: Edward Elgar, 1993.

Jap, Sandy D., Chris Manolis, and Barton A. Weitz. "Relationship Quality in Buyer-Seller Interactions in Channels of Distribution." *Journal of Business Research* 46, no. 3 (1999): 202–13.

John, George, and Barton A. Weitz. "Forward Integration into Distribution: An Empirical Test of Transaction Cost Analysis." *Journal of Law, Economics, and Organization* 4, no. 2 (1988): 337–55.

Jones, Peter. "Managing Hospitality Innovation." *Cornell Hotel and Restaurant Administration Quarterly* 37, no. 5 (1996): 86.

Joshi, Ashwin W. "How and Why Do Relatively Dependent Manufacturers Resist Supplier Power?" *Journal of Marketing Theory and Practice* 6, no. 4 (1998): 61–77.

Joskow, Paul L. "Contract Duration and Relationship-Specific Investments: Empirical Evidence from Coal Markets." *American Economic Review* 77, no. 1 (1987): 168–85.

Kapferer, Jean-Noel. *Strategic Brand Management.* New York: Free Press, 1992.

Kasulis, Jack J., and Robert E. Spekman. "A Framework for the Use of Power." *European Journal of Marketing* 14, no. 4 (1980): 180–91.

Kaufmann, Patrick J., and Rajiv P. Dant. "The Dimensions of Commercial Exchange." *Marketing Letters* 3, no. 2 (1992): 171–85

Kaufmann, Patrick J., and Louis W. Stern, "Relational Exchange Norms, Perceptions of Unfairness, and Retained Hostility in Commercial Litigation." *Journal of Conflict Resolution* 32, no. 3 (1988): 534–52.

Keller, Kevin Lane. "Conceptualizing, Measuring, and Managing Customer-Based Brand Equity." Working paper, Marketing Science Institute, Cambridge, MA, October 1991.

———. *Strategic Brand Management: Building, Measuring, and Managing Brand Equity.* New York: Prentice-Hall, 1997.

———. *Strategic Brand Management: Building, Measuring, and Managing Brand Equity.* 3rd ed. Upper Saddle River, NJ: Prentice-Hall, 2008.

Kim, Byung-Do, and Mary W. Sullivan. "The Effect of Parent Brand Experience on Line Extension Trial and Repeat Purchase." *Marketing Letters* 9, no. 2 (1998): 181–93.

Kimes, Sheryl E. "The Basics of Yield Management." *Cornell Hospitality and Restaurant Administration Quarterly* 30, no. 3 (1989): 14–19.

Kogut, Bruce, and Ugo Zander. "Knowledge of the Firm, Combinative Capabilities, and the Replication of Technology." *Organization Science* 3, no. 3 (1992): 383–97.

———. "Knowledge of the Firm and the Evolutionary Theory of the Multinational Corporation." *Journal of International Business Studies* 24, no. 4 (1993): 625–46.

Kohli, Ajay K., and Bernard Jaworski. "Market Orientation: The Construct, Research Propositions, and Managerial Implications." *Journal of Marketing* 54, no. 2 (1990): 1–18.

Kotler, Philip, John T. Bowen, and James Makens. *Marketing for Hospitality and Tourism*. 5th ed. Upper Saddle River, NJ: Pearson Prentice Hall, 2009.

Kumar, Nirmalya, and Lisa K. Scheer, "The Effects of Perceived Interdependence on Dealer Attitudes." *Journal of Marketing Research* 32, no. 3 (1995): 348–56.

———. "The Effects of Supplier Fairness on Vulnerable Resellers." *Journal of Marketing Research* 32, no. 1 (1995): 54–65.

Kumar, Nirmalya, Louis W. Stern, and Ravi S. Achrol. "Assessing Reseller Performance from the Perspective of the Supplier." *Journal of Marketing Research* 29, no. 2 (1992): 238–53.

Labagh, Richard, and Jonathan D. Barsky. "A Strategy for Customer Satisfaction." *Cornell Hospitality and Restaurant Administration Quarterly* 33, no. 5 (1992): 32–40.

Lam, Alice. "Embedded Firms, Embedded Knowledge: Problems of Collaboration and Knowledge Transfer in Global Cooperative Ventures." *Organization Studies* 18, no. 6 (1997): 973–96.

Lee, Denny. "Extreme Makeover: Taking High Style to the High Seas." *New York Times,* February 26, 2006, T8.

Leuthesser, Lance. "Defining, Measuring, and Managing Brand Equity." Conference summary. Marketing Science Institute, Cambridge, MA, May 1988.

Lewis, Robert C. "Advertising Your Hotel's Position." *Cornell Hotel and Restaurant Administration Quarterly* 31, no. 2 (1990): 85.

———. "The Market Position: Mapping Guests' Perceptions of Hotel Operations." *Cornell Hotel and Restaurant Administration Quarterly* 26, no. 2 (1985): 88–89.

———. "The Positioning Statement for Hotels." *Cornell Hotel and Restaurant Administration Quarterly* 22, no. 1 (1981): 53.

———. "When Guests Complain." *Cornell Hotel and Restaurant Administration Quarterly* 24, no. 2 (1983): 23–32.

Lewis, Robert C., and Richard E. Chambers. *Marketing Leadership in Hospitality: Foundations and Practices.* New York: Van Nostrand Reinhold, 1989.

Lewis, Robert C., Richard E. Chambers, and Harsha E. Chacko. *Marketing Leadership in Hospitality: Foundations and Practices.* 2nd ed. New York: Van Nostrand Reinhold, 1995.

Lohita, Ritu, Charles M. Brooks, and Robert E. Krapfel. "What Constitutes a Transaction-Specific Asset? An Examination of the Dimensions and Types." *Journal of Business Research* 30, no. 3 (1994): 261–70.

Loken, Barbara, and Deborah R. John, "Diluting Brand Beliefs: When Do Brand Extensions Have a Negative Impact?" *Journal of Marketing* 57, no. 3 (1993), 71–84.

Lowrey, Annie. "Are Group Buying and Coupon Deal Companies Like Groupon and Livingsocial in for a Bubble?" *Washington Post,* January 16, 2011.

Luo, Yadong. *Entry and Cooperative Strategies in International Business Expansion.* Westport, CT: Quorum Books, 1999.

Lusch, Robert F., and James R. Brown. "Interdependency, Contracting, and Relational Behavior in Marketing Channels." *Journal of Marketing* 60, no. 4 (1996): 19–38.

———. "A Modified Model of Power in the Marketing Channel." *Journal of Marketing Research* 19, no. 3 (1982): 312–23.

Lyons, Bruce. "Barriers to Entry." In *Economics of Industrial Organization* (Surveys in Economics), ed. Stephen Davies and Bruce Lyons with Huw Dixon and Paul Geroski, 26–72. New York: Longman Group UK, 1988.

Macneil, Ian R. *The New Social Contract.* New Haven, CT: Yale University Press, 1980.

Madhok, Anoop. "Cost, Value, and Foreign Market Entry Mode: The Transaction and the Firm." *Strategic Management Journal* 18, no. 1 (1997): 39–61.

Malley, Mike. "Getting the Most Value out of Franchising." *Hotel and Motel Management* (supplement) 212, no. 8 (1997): 31–32.

McCarthy, Jon M., and Lori E. Raleigh. "Evaluating Franchise and Chain Affiliation Programs." In *Hotel Asset Management: Principles and Practices,* ed. Paul Beals and Greg Denton, 117–36. Lansing, MI: Educational Institute of the American Hotel Motel and Lodging Association, 2003.

Mishra, Debi Pradad, Jan B. Heide, and Stanton G. Cort. "Information Asymmetry and Levels of Agency Relationships." *Journal of Marketing Research* 35, no. 3 (1998): 277–95.

Mohr, Jakki, and John. R. Nevin. "Communication Strategies in Marketing Channels: A Theoretical Perspective." *Journal of Marketing* 54, no. 4 (1990): 36–51.

Mohr, Jakki J., and Ravipreet S. Sohi. "Communication Flows in Distribution Channels: Impact on Assessments of Communication Quality and Satisfaction." *Journal of Retailing* 71, no. 4 (1995): 393–416.

Morgan, Michael S. "Traveler's Choice: The Effects of Advertising and Prior Stay." *Cornell Hotel and Restaurant Administration Quarterly* 32, no. 4 (1991): 40–49.

Morgan, Michael S., and Chekitan S. Dev. "An Empirical Study of Brand Switching for a Retail Service." *Journal of Retailing* 70, no. 3 (1994): 267–82.

Morgan, Robert M., and Shelby D. Hunt. "The Commitment-Trust Theory of Relationship Marketing." *Journal of Marketing* 58, no. 3 (1994): 20–28.

Morton, William. "Closing the Marketing Gap." *Cornell Hotel and Restaurant Administration Quarterly* 7, no. 4 (1967): 9–16.

Narver, John C., and Stanley F. Slater. "The Effect of a Market Orientation on Business Profitability." *Journal of Marketing* 54, no. 4 (1990): 20–35.

neXtup Research. "Groupon Anxiety." *Economist,* March 19, 2011.

Noordwier, Thomas G., George John, and John R. Nevin. "Performance Outcomes of Purchasing Arrangements in Industrial Buyer-Vendor Relationships." *Journal of Marketing* 54, no. 4 (1990): 80–93.

O'Connor, Peter, and Andrew J. Frew. "The Future of Hotel Electronic Distribution: Expert and Industry Perspectives." *Cornell Hotel and Restaurant Administration Quarterly* 43, no. 2 (2002): 33–45.

Orkin, Eric B. "Boosting Your Bottom Line with Yield Management." *Cornell Hospitality and Restaurant Administration Quarterly* 28, no. 4 (1988): 52–56.

Ottenbacher, Michael, and B. Gray. "The New Service Development Process: The Initial Stages for Hotel Innovations." *FIU Hospitality Review* 22, no. 2 (2004): 59–70.

Ottenbacher, Michael C., Vivienne Shaw, and M. Howley. "Impact of Employee Management on Hospitality Innovation Success." *FIU Hospitality and Tourism Review* 23, no. 1 (2005): 82–95.

Overstreet, George. "Creating Value in Oversupplied Markets: The Case of Charlottesville, Virginia, Hotels." *Cornell Hotel and Restaurant Administration Quarterly* 34, no. 5 (1993): 84–91.

Pan, Yigang, and David K. Tse. "The Hierarchical Model of Market Entry Modes." *Journal of International Business Studies* 31, no. 4 (2000): 535–54.

Parsa, H. G., "Franchisor-Franchisee Relationships in Quick-Service-Restaurant Systems." *Cornell Hotel and Restaurant Administration Quarterly* 37, no. 3 (1996): 42–49.

Payan, Janice M., and Richard G. McFarland. "Decomposing Influence Strategies: Argument Structure and Dependence as Determinants of the Effectiveness of Influence Strategies in Gaining Channel Member Compliance." *Journal of Marketing* 69, no. 3 (2005): 66–79.

Payan, Janice M., and John R. Nevin. "Influence Strategy Efficacy in Supplier-Distributor Relationships." *Journal of Business Research* 59, no. 4 (2006): 457–65.

Peng, Mike W., and Peggy Sue Heath. "The Growth of the Firm in Planned Economies in Transition: Institutions, Organizations, and Strategic Choice." *Academy of Management Review* 21, no. 2 (1996): 492–528.

Peng, Mike W., and Y. Luo. "Managerial Ties and Firm Performance in a Transition Economy: The Nature of a Micro-Macro Link." *Academy of Management Journal* 43, no. 3 (2000): 486–501.

Perkins, Ed. "How to Navigate Travel Flash Sale Sites." *USA Today Travel,* August 24, 2011. http://travel.usatoday.com/deals/inside/story/2011–08–25/How-to-navigate-travel-flash-sale-sites/50125442/1 (accessed September 5, 2011).

Peters, Clarence H. "Pre-opening Market Analysis for Hotels." *Cornell Hospitality and Restaurant Administration Quarterly* 19, no. 1 (1978): 15–22.

Pfeffer, Jeffrey, and Gerald R. Salancik. *The External Control of Organizations: A Resource Dependence Perspective.* New York: Harper and Row, 1978.

Prasad, Kesh, and Chekitan Dev. "Model Estimates of Financial Impact of Guest Satisfaction Efforts." *Hotel and Motel Management* 217, no. 14 (2002): 23.

Provan, Keith G., and Steven J. Skinner. "Interorganizational Dependence and Control as Predictors of Opportunism in Dealer-Supplier Relations." *Academy of Management Journal* 32, no. 1 (1989): 202–12.

Ramond, Charles. "Advertising Research for the Food Service Industry." *Cornell Hotel and Restaurant Administration Quarterly* 18, no. 1 (1977): 20–32.

Ramsay, J. O. "Some Statistical Approaches to Multidimensional Scaling." *Journal of the Royal Statistical Society,* ser. A, 145, no. 3 (1982): 285–312.

Ross, Barbara-Jean, Chekitan S. Dev, and Kathleen M. Dennison. "Carnival Cruise Lines." In *Strategic Management Cases: Instructor's Manual,* ed. D. W. Grigsby and M. J. Stahl, 71–76. Belmont, CA: Wadsworth, 1993.

Relihan, Walter J. "The Yield Management Approach to Hotel-Room Pricing." *Cornell Hospitality and Restaurant Administration Quarterly* 30, no. 1 (1989): 40–45.

Rubin, Paul. *Managing Business Transactions.* New York: Free Press, 1990.

Rushmore, Stephen. "Hotel Franchising: How to Be a Successful Franchisee." *Real Estate Journal,* Summer 1997, 56.

Rusli, Evelyn M. "With Eye on Public Offering, Coupons.com Attracts Big Investments." *New York Times,* June 9, 2011.

Saba, Jennifer, and Clare Baldwin. "Groupon Worth $25 Billion? Nope." Reuters (March, 15, 2011).

Saporito, Bill. "The Groupon Clipper." *Time,* February 21, 2011.

Schegg, Roland, Susanne Frey, Jamie Murphy, and Doina Olaru. "Swiss Hotels' Web-site and E-mail Management: The Bandwagon Effect." *Cornell Hotel and Restaurant Administration Quarterly* 44, no. 1 (2003): 71–87.

Schurr, Paul H., and Julie L. Ozanne. "Influences on Exchange Processes: Buyer's Preconceptions of a Seller's Trustworthiness and Bargaining Toughness." *Journal of Consumer Research* 11, no. 4 (1985): 939–53.

Shane, Scott A. "Hybrid Organizational Arrangements and Their Implications for Firm Growth and Survival: A Study of New Franchisors." *Academy of Management Journal* 39, no. 1 (1996): 216–34.

Sharkey, Joe. "At High-End Hotels, Business Is Looking Up." *New York Times,* May 11, 2010, B6.

Srivastava, Rajendra K., and Allan Shocker. "Brand Equity: A Perspective on Its Meaning and Measurement." Technical working paper. Marketing Science Institute, Cambridge, MA, October 1991.

Steiner, Christopher. "The Next Web Phenom." *Forbes,* August 30, 2010, 58–62.

Stoddard, James E., Janet E. Keith, and James R. Brown. "The Measurement of Influence Strategies in Distribution Channels: Scale Development and Testing." *Journal of Marketing Channels* 7, no. 4 (2000): 83–108.

Stump, Rodney L., and Jan B. Heide. "Controlling Supplier Opportunism in Industrial Relationships." *Journal of Marketing Research* 33, no. 4 (1996): 431–41.

Sturman, Michael C. "Using Your Pay System to Improve Employee Performance—How You Pay Makes a Difference." *Cornell Hospitality Reports* (Cornell Center for Hospitality Research) 6, no. 13 (2006).

Suskind, Alex M. "An Examination of Guest Complaints and Complaint Communication Channels—the Medium Does Matter." *Cornell Hospitality Reports* (Cornell Center for Hospitality Research) 6, no. 14 (2006).

Swan, Philip. "Raging Belmonte." *Lodging* 70, no. 10 (1992): 28–29.

Swinyard, William R. "A Research Approach to Restaurant Marketing." *Cornell Hotel and Restaurant Administration Quarterly* 17, no. 4 (1977): 56–61.

Talbott, Barbara. "The Power of Personal Service." *Cornell Hospitality Industry Perspectives* (Cornell Center for Hospitality Research). White paper. 2006. http://www.hotelschool.cornell.edu/chr/pdf/showpdf/chr/industry/

powerpersonalservice.pdf?t=CHR&my_path_info=chr/industry/
powerpersonalservice.pdf (accessed February 1, 2012).

Tauber, Edward. "Brand Leverage: Study for Growth in a Cost-Controlled World." *Journal of Advertising Research*. 28, no. 4 (1988): 26–30.

Teece, David J., "Capturing Value from Knowledge Assets: The New Economy, Markets for Know-How, and Intangible Assets." *California Management Review* 40, no. 3 (1998): 55–79.

Victorino, Liana, Rohit Verma, Gerhard Plaschka, and Chekitan Dev. "Service Innovation and Customer Choices in the Hospitality Industry." *Managing Service Quality* 15, no. 6 (2005): 555–76.

Wathne, Kenneth H., and Jan B. Heide. "Opportunism in Interfirm Relationships: Forms, Outcomes, and Solutions." *Journal of Marketing* 64, no. 4 (2000): 36–51.

Weiss, Bari. "Groupon's $6 Billion Gambler." *Wall Street Journal,* December 18, 2010.

Williamson, Oliver E. *The Economic Institutions of Capitalism—Firms, Markets, Relational Contracting.* New York: Free Press, 1985.

——. *Markets and Hierarchies: Analysis and Anti-trust Implications.* New York: Free Press, 1975.

Winer, Russell S. "A Reference Price Model of Brand Choice for Frequently Purchased Products." *Journal of Consumer Research* 13, no. 2 (1986): 250–56.

Woong, Wailing. "Gap's Groupon Pulls in $11 Million." *Chicago Tribune,* August 20, 2010.

Yesawich, Peter C. "The Execution and Measurement of a Marketing Program." *Cornell Hospitality and Restaurant Administration Quarterly* 20, no. 1 (1979): 41–52.

——. "Post-opening Market Analysis for Hotels." *Cornell Hospitality and Restaurant Administration Quarterly* 19, no. 3 (1978): 70–81.

Yoshihashi, Pauline. "Hotel Recovery Will Be a Late Arrival." *Wall Street Journal,* July 27, 1992, B1.

Yüksel, Atila, and Mike Rimmington. "Customer-Satisfaction Measurement: Performance Counts." *Cornell Hospitality and Restaurant Administration Quarterly* 39, no. 6 (1998): 60–70.